Theology
of the Body

IN CONTEXT

Genesis and Growth

By William E. May

Pauline
BOOKS & MEDIA
Boston

Library of Congress Cataloging-in-Publication Data

May, William E., 1928–
    Theology of the body in context : genesis and growth / by William E. May.
        p. cm.
    ISBN 0-8198-7431-0 (pbk.)
    1. John Paul II, Pope, 1920–2005. Theology of the body 2.   Human body—
Religious aspects—Catholic Church. 3.   Sex—Religious aspects—Catholic Church.
4. Catholic Church—Doctrines. I. Title.
    BX1795.B63M28 2010
    233'.5—dc22

                                                            2010001472

The Scripture quotations contained herein are from the *New Revised Standard Version Bible: Catholic Edition*, copyright © 1989, 1993, Division of Christian Education of the National Council of the Churches of Christ in the United States of America. Used by permission. All rights reserved.

Chapter three is a revised and expanded version of previously published material. Substantive portions were published in William May's book *Marriage: The Rock on Which the Family Is Built*, second edition, Ignatius Press, and are used here with permission.

Quotations from Pope John Paul II used with the permission of the Libreria Editrice Vaticana, 00120, Città del Vaticana.

We acknowledge and thank those publishers whose material, whether in the public domain or under copyright protection, has made this work possible. Every effort has been made to obtain all the proper permissions. But if we have inadvertently not obtained a required permission, we ask the publisher to contact the editor for proper acknowledgment and compensation.

Cover design by Rosana Usselmann

Cover photo: Ewa Mucha / istockphoto.com

Published by Pauline Books & Media, 50 Saint Pauls Avenue, Boston, MA 02130-3491

Printed in the U.S.A.

www.pauline.org

Pauline Books & Media is the publishing house of the Daughters of St. Paul, an international congregation of women religious serving the Church with the communications media.

1 2 3 4 5 6 7 8 9   14 13 12 11 10

To my wife of fifty-one years,
God's great gift to me,
Patricia Ann Keck May

Contents

Introduction

This book seeks to summarize the rich and comprehensive teaching of Pope John Paul II on the person, marriage, and family. Even before he became pope, Karol Wojtyla devoted considerable attention to these questions in plays such as *The Jeweler's Shop*, *Our God's Brother*, and *The Radiation of Fatherhood*. He wrote an important book on the subject of family in Polish in 1960, which was translated into English in 1981 under the title *Love and Responsibility*.[1]

From the time he became pope in 1978, John Paul II devoted much of his considerable energy to thinking, writing, and speaking on the person, marriage, and family. From September 1979 through November 1984 he gave a remarkable series of Wednesday audiences devoted to the "Theology of the Body," marriage, and human sexuality. In response to the 1980 Synod of Bishops devoted to the role of the Christian family, he issued his masterful apostolic exhortation "The Role of the Christian Family in the Modern World" (*Familiaris Consortio*), surely one of the most important magisterial documents ever promulgated on the person, marriage, and the family. In 1988, on the occasion of the Marian Year, he issued his apostolic letter *Mulieris Dignitatem* ("The Dignity and Vocation of Women"), sections of which beautifully summarize major ideas developed in the "Theology of the Body" and deepen his reflections on the man-woman relationship. In early 1994 he published his beautiful *Letter to Families* as a contribution to the International Year of the Family, another document beautifully summarizing major ideas of the "Theology of the Body." In addition, every year of his pontificate from October 16, 1978, through April 2, 2005, witnessed hundreds of addresses devoted to the person, marriage, and the family, given throughout the world to a wide range of audiences. Thousands of pages in the many volumes of the *Insegnamenti di Giovanni Paolo II* published by the Vatican are devoted to this teaching. He can surely be regarded as one of the greatest champions of the human person, marriage, and the family of all time.

In addition, in 1981 John Paul II founded the Pontificio Istituto Giovanni Paolo II per Studi su Matrimonio e Famiglia at the Pontifical Lateran University in Rome. In 1988 he founded the American session of the Pontifical John Paul II Institute for Studies on Marriage and Family in Washington, D.C. In 1991 I was named the Michael J. McGivney Professor of Moral Theology at this institute for graduate studies in theology, focused on marriage and the family. Since then I have regularly taught courses in the various graduate programs the institute offers. These courses have covered in depth John Paul's teaching on the person, marriage, and the family, and through the years I have grown in my appreciation for the work he has done. The writings of Karol Wojtyla/John Paul II are indeed profound; some are difficult to understand in parts and certainly challenge the reader. This is perhaps particularly true of *Love and Responsibility* and the addresses on the "Theology of the Body." I believe I have now read *Love and Responsibility* at least twenty times; each time I discover something new and important. Many times students have helped me come to a better grasp of certain texts.

John Paul's addresses on the "Theology of the Body" (hereafter TOB) present the culmination and living core of his thought on the person, marriage, and the family that began with his doctoral study of the theology of Saint John of the Cross, developed and deepened in *Love and Responsibility*, and ultimately found fullest expression in TOB. Michael Waldstein points out that Karol Wojtyla's/John Paul II's point of departure as a theologian is the "spousal" personalism of Saint John of the Cross:

> Saint John of the Cross does not thematically discuss love between man and woman. Yet, his frequent use of bride-bridegroom imagery contains a rich implicit theology of marriage inspired above all by the Song of Songs. In *Love and Responsibility*, Wojtyla makes this implicit theology of marriage explicit, enriching it by further insight.... [T]he core of Wojtyla's philosophical concern in *Love and Responsibility* is the understanding of the gift of self as the key element of spousal love.... [T]he spousal theology of Saint John of the Cross ultimately shapes the agenda of *Love and Responsibility*.[2]

In this book I want to show how *Love and Responsibility*, a profound, challenging, and difficult work, helps prepare the way for TOB. I will then show how the teaching found in *Familiaris Consortio*, written when TOB was about halfway completed, embraces many of TOB's key ideas and themes. I will conclude by considering two documents written after TOB was completed, the apostolic letters *Mulieris Dignitatem* and *Letter to Families*. I will thus take up the writings in this order: (1) *Love and Responsibility*, (2) *Familiaris Consortio*,

(3) *Theology of the Body*, and (4) *Mulieris Dignitatem* and *Letter to Families*.

The chapter on the theology of the body has been written in light of Michael Waldstein's new translation and superb introduction to John Paul II's catecheses on this subject in *Man and Woman He Created Them: A Theology of the Body*.[3] It was my privilege to serve as the *censor deputatus* to grant the *nihil obstat* for this magnificent publication. It has also been my privilege to serve in the same capacity for the revised edition of Christopher West's *The Theology of the Body Explained: A Commentary on John Paul II's "Gospel of the Body,"* with a foreword by Michael Waldstein.[4]

CHAPTER 1

Karol Wojtyla's *Love and Responsibility*: Themes Relevant to the Theology of the Body

Karol Wojtyla wrote *Love and Responsibility* to give spiritual and moral advice to his students at the Catholic University of Lublin. In fact, it was given its first form, prior to publication in 1960, as a series of lectures to these students in 1958–59. Wojtyla was a celibate priest. In his introduction to the first edition he writes:

> It is sometimes said that only those who live a conjugal life can pronounce on the subject of marriage, and only those who have experienced it can pronounce on love between man and woman. In this view ... priests and persons living a celibate life can have nothing to say on questions of love and marriage.

He notes that in his pastoral work a priest often encounters the problems facing men and women seeking to live good lives, and spouses who are doing their best to be good husbands and wives. He then says that is how the book came about, as a constant confrontation of doctrine, i.e., Catholic teaching on sexual morality and marriage, and life. His purpose is to show why this teaching is true and rooted in the truth about human persons and the goods that fulfill them (see *Love and Responsibility*, pp. 15–16).

Published in Polish in 1960 and in English in 1981, *Love and Responsibility* has five chapters:

CHAPTER 1: The Person and the Sexual Urge
CHAPTER 2: The Person and Love
CHAPTER 3: The Person and Chastity
CHAPTER 4: Justice Toward the Creator
CHAPTER 5: Sexology and Ethics

I will summarize material from these chapters central to John Paul II's teaching that I believe are relevant to his "Theology of the Body," where his magnificent, faith-filled, and philosophically and theologically rooted teaching on the human person, marriage, and family finds its richest and fullest expression. I will note those sections of TOB in which I believe the ideas and themes set forth in *Love and Responsibility* are developed.

Love and Responsibility, Chapter 1: The Person and the Sexual Urge

Six ideas found in this chapter are crucial:

1. A human person is *never* to be used merely as a means to an end of another person.

2. One major way of "using persons" in this way, particularly in the realm of sex, is to use them as a means of experiencing pleasure.

3. Love between persons demands a *common good*, as illustrated by the love between man and woman in marriage.

4. The command to love is rooted in the *personalistic norm* and its requirements.

5. Every human person is a sexual being, and by reason of his "sexual urge" is dynamically oriented from within toward a person of the opposite sex.

6. The "sexual urge" has an "existential dimension" by which it is ordered to the preservation of men, of human persons.

Each of these ideas is deepened and enriched immeasurably by Wojtyla/John Paul II's TOB.

1. A Human Person Is Never to Be Used Merely as a Means to an End of Another Person

Your Dictionary Online (http://www.yourdictionary. com) defines "to use" in its first and basic definition as: "to put or bring into action or service; employ for or apply to a given purpose." This seems to me to be the basic sense in which Wojtyla uses the expression. There is a legitimate sense in which human persons do "use" other persons as means to eternal ends; for example, a basketball coach "uses" some individual human persons as players in a game, and he freely substitutes other human persons for different players during the game. There is nothing wrong in this. What is always gravely wrong is for one human person to "use" another human person *merely* as a means to some end, ignoring the truth that human persons, precisely because they are persons, are never to be used in this way. An example is a medical scientist using human persons as subjects without their free and informed consent in experiments that could be harmful to them. Wojtyla insists that, as *persons*, human beings are totally different from other animals because they have an "inner self" and "interior life," and as such are irreplaceable and nonsubstitutable (pp. 22–23). He affirms that "a child, even an unborn child, cannot be denied personality in its most objective ontological sense, although it is true that it has yet to acquire, step by step, many of the traits which will make it psychologically and ethically a distinct personality" (p. 26). This is most important: unborn children, still in the embryonic or fetal stage of development, are indeed persons while in their mothers' wombs and do not *become* persons at some later stage of development.

In his "Theology of the Body," Pope John Paul II richly develops the truth that all human beings, from conception until natural death, are "persons" as the ethical significance of an important truth: that the human body reveals the human person who is made in the image and likeness of God and is a being who is to be loved and whose vocation is to love. Thus in TOB 5–7 he beautifully develops what can be called man's "existential" solitude, his solitude as the only visibly created being who is "alone before God." Moreover, it is through his awareness of his own body that man realizes he is "other than" the other animals in being alone before God, whose living image he is. This solitude is even deeper than the solitude of the male-person vis-à-vis the female-person. Man, male and female, is "alone" with God because only man realizes that he is "the only creature on earth which God willed for itself" (*Gaudium et Spes*, 24). To put this truth another way, man, male and female, realizes that he is the only animal who is a "person." He is, as it were, the "created word" that the Uncreated Word, the only-begotten Son of the Father, became precisely to show us how deeply God loves us.

2. One Major Way of "Using Persons" This Way, Particularly in the Realm of Sex, Is to Use Them as a Means of Experiencing Pleasure

"To use" also means "to enjoy or experience pleasure," and frequently, particularly in the realm of sex, human persons are "used" as the source of pleasure and enjoyment. Here sexual morality comes into play. One person can make pleasure the aim of his activity by using another person as a means of obtaining pleasure. To do so is to treat the person not as he or she is — an utterly irreplaceable and nonsubstitutable person — but rather as a "thing," a commodity meant to satisfy desires. Thus a man uses a woman in this way, even his own wife, if he has sex with her *only* because her body can be used to satisfy his sexual desires without even caring that the "body" satisfying his lust is the body of his own wife. However, "the belief that a human being is a person leads to the acceptance of the postulate that enjoyment must be subordinated to love" (p. 34).

In TOB 8–10 John Paul II beautifully shows the original unity, one of love, between the first man and woman, and in TOB 13.5 and following he develops what he calls "the spousal meaning" of the human body in its masculinity/femininity, which shows that the man in his very bodiliness is meant to be a "gift" to the woman and she in her very bodiliness to be a "gift" to the man. In getting married a man and a woman "give" themselves to each other and "receive" one another as irreplaceable, nonsubstitutable, and nondisposable persons. And they do so precisely as bodily persons whose bodies are integral to their being as man and woman. Their bodies have a "spousal" meaning or significance, i.e., the man's body is a sign that he is meant to be a gift to his wife, and her body is a sign that she is to be a gift to her husband. Non-married men and women who engage in fornication or adultery are in principle replaceable, substitutable, and disposable. Rather than "giving" their bodies to one another they simply "lend" them to each other as long as each gets pleasure from doing so.

3. Love Between Persons Demands a Common Good Among Persons, as Illustrated in the Love Between Man and Woman in Marriage

Commitment to a common good unites and distinguishes a real *community of persons* from a disorganized mob or crowd. Thus an *academic community*, composed essentially of teachers and students and assisted by administration and staff, has as its common good the good of learning, to which faculty and students and staff are committed. A larger and greater common good is what makes our nation united and one: *e pluribus unum*. The citizens of our country hold certain truths as central, to which they dedicate themselves (see the *Declaration of Independence*). And commitment to a common good is, as Wojtyla argues, necessary for *love* between a man and a woman to flourish.

"'Love' is the opposite of 'using,'" and love is the only proper attitude to have toward a person. But love is possible only if there is a "bond of a *common good*" uniting persons. Indeed, "Man's capacity for love depends on his willingness consciously to seek a good together with others, and to subordinate himself to that good for the sake of others, or to others for the sake of that good. *Love is exclusively the portion of human persons*" (pp. 28–29). Wojtyla applies this to marriage, one of the most important areas where the principle that love is possible only if there is some common good is applicable. In marriage, "a man and a woman are united in such a way that they become in a sense 'one flesh,' ... i.e., one common subject, as it were, of sexual life." To ensure that they do not become mere means in each other's eyes

> they must share the same end. Such an end, where marriage is concerned, is procreation, the future generation, a family,

and, at the same time, the continual ripening of the relation-ship between two people, in all the areas of activity which conjugal life includes. (p. 30)

This is shown by the commitment a man and a woman make when they "give" themselves to each other and receive each other in marriage. In doing so they commit themselves irrevocably to one another by committing themselves to mar-riage — a lifelong and intimate covenant of love and life, and to its "goods," i.e., faithful spousal love, the gift of children, the effort to help each other grow in holiness.

In considering the man-woman relationship in its widest sense, Wojtyla maintains that the love he is talking about "is identified with a particular readiness to subordinate oneself to that good, which ... the value of the person represents, re-gardless of difference of sex" (p. 31). In other words, the value of the person is the ultimate "common good" uniting men and women in love.

John Paul II richly develops the meaning of marriage in TOB 87–117. He takes up in depth the meaning of marriage as a sacrament and of the human body, male and female, as a special gift in this sacrament. What "makes" marriage is the free and irrevocable consent of the man and the woman to give and receive each other as wife and husband and to pur-sue the "common good" of marriage. Their marriage is sacra-mental if the man and the woman are baptized, i.e., irrevocably joined to Christ through baptism for weal or woe; and in baptism they commit themselves to the "common good" of the triune God and of his adopted children in Christ, i.e., holiness. This matter will be taken up in depth in the chapter on John Paul's theology of the body.

4. The Command to Love Is Rooted in the "Personalistic Norm" and Its Requirements

Wojtyla begins the section on the personalistic norm by declaring: "The commandment laid down in the New Testament demands from man love for others, for his neighbors — in the fullest sense, then, love for persons. For God, whom the commandment to love names first, is the most perfect personal Being." He continues by saying that the utilitarian principle, which makes pleasure the highest good and "uses" persons as mere means to attain this end, is utterly incompatible with the commandment to love. He then says:

> But it becomes obvious that if the commandment to love, and the love which is the object of this commandment, are to have any meaning, we must find a basis for them other than the utilitarian premise and the utilitarian system of values. This can only be the personalistic principle and the personalistic norm. (pp. 40–41)

But what is this norm? Wojtyla formulates it negatively and positively:

> This norm, in its negative aspect, states that the person is the kind of good which does not admit of use and cannot be treated as an object of use and as such the means to an end. In its positive form the personalist norm confirms this: the person is a good towards which the only proper and adequate attitude is love. (p. 41)

The personalistic norm, in its negative aspect, is easily illustrated. A man, for example, cannot use a woman's body as a commodity to be consumed, as it were, merely as an object capable of giving him pleasure. This is to treat her not as the kind of being she is, a person, but as a mere thing. In its positive aspect it can be illustrated in many ways; for instance, a good basketball coach does not treat his players as mere individuals or things he can use to win a game. Rather, he treats them as the kind of beings they are, persons who are irreplaceable, nonsubstitutable, nondisposable. He may substitute players as individuals in the game and not be using them as mere disposable or substitutable things, for he respects them as irreplaceable persons whom he must love. He respects them as persons in whom he wills that the true goods of human existence flourish, and one of these goods is the development of one's skills in play and work.

For to love a person is to love and respect the *goods* meant to flourish in him or her, for instance life itself, bodily integrity and health, knowledge of the truth, friendship with others, and marriage, and to be unwilling intentionally to damage, destroy, or impede these goods of human persons. This point is later developed by John Paul II in his encyclical *Veritatis Splendor*, in particular in numbers 12 and following.

He further develops this in TOB in many places where he shows the *ethical significance* of the body. Perhaps of special significance is TOB 24.3, where he makes it clear that our Lord's Sermon on the Mount fulfills and perfects the law of love. Indeed the whole of TOB 24–63, devoted to an analysis of the Sermon on the Mount and Christ's words about concupiscent desire and Saint Paul's teaching on purity of heart, provides an extensive and profound development of this theme of *Love and Responsibility*. In those catecheses of TOB the Pope is seeking to show how both our Lord and Saint Paul were appealing to the human heart. John Paul was contrasting two types of persons: the concupiscent person, who exemplifies the utilitarian principle and scale of values, and the person who, precisely because of Christ's redemptive act and his participation in it, has come into possession of concupiscent desires, is not possessed by them, and is capable of giving himself away in love to other persons.

5. Every Human Person Is a Sexual Being, and by Reason of His Sexual Urge Is Dynamically Oriented from Within Toward a Person of the Opposite Sex

No one can doubt that human persons are sexual beings. After all, human persons are either male or female, with their masculinity and femininity, and no one thinks it odd that men find women physically attractive precisely because they are women with their feminine sexuality, and vice versa. Human beings are, as it were, naturally inclined to be attracted to persons of the opposite sex not only because of their sexual attributes but also as concrete men and women. But precisely what does all this mean? Wojtyla probes the matter deeply in the great attention he devoted to what he calls the sexual urge, in a section of chapter 1 of *Love and Responsibility*. This section is immeasurably deepened by the analyses he provides in his TOB. Wojtyla considers the sexual *urge* as "a *natural drive born in all human beings, a vector of aspiration* along which their whole existence develops and perfects itself from within" (p. 46). He emphasizes that every human being is a sexual being: "membership of one of the two sexes means that a person's whole existence has a particular orientation which shows itself in his or her actual internal development" (p. 47). He says the sexual urge is not fully defined as an orientation toward the sexual attributes of the other sex as such: rather it is directed "towards another human being ... [and] if it is directed towards the sexual attributes as such this must be recognized as an impoverishment or even a perversion of the urge" (e.g., considering women merely as "playgirls" and men as "playboys," homosexuality, and bestiality). He then says:

> The natural direction of the sexual urge is towards a human being of the other sex and not merely towards "the other sex"

as such. It is just because it is directed towards a particular human being that the sexual urge can provide the framework within which, and the basis on which, the possibility of love arises.... The sexual urge in man has a natural tendency to develop into love simply because the two objects affected ... are both people.... [But love is] given its definitive shape by *acts of will at the level of the person*.... The sexual urge in man ... is naturally subordinate to the will, and *ipso facto* subject to the specific dynamics of that freedom which the will possesses. (pp. 49–50)

Because of this dimension of the sexual urge, a male human person is naturally attracted to a female human person and vice versa. Each person experiences this attraction, nor are people surprised when they observe it taking place.

Pope John Paul II offers a magnificently rich development of this material especially in TOB 13–19, where he reflects profoundly on the "spousal meaning of the body" in the state of original innocence, a meaning that was, as it were, "veiled" but never lost as a result of the fall, and in a somewhat different way in TOB 103–107 when he analyzes the "language of the body." This will be shown more fully in the chapter on the theology of the body.

6. The Sexual Urge Has an Existential Dimension by which It Is Ordered to the Preservation of the Existence of Men, of Human Persons

What is the ultimate reason why the human species is divided into male and female? The short answer is that for the species to continue, new human beings, new human persons, must come into existence. They do only because of the sexual complementarity of male and female. Our digestive, circulatory, and nervous systems, for example, function in each of us individually, whether we are male or female. But we can exercise our procreative powers only with a person of the opposite sex. And unless we exercise them our species would die out. This matter is taken up magnificently by Wojtyla in *Love and Responsibility*.

Wojtyla emphasizes that the ultimate *end* of the sexual urge is "something supra-personal, the existence of the species *Homo*, the constant prolongation of its existence" (p. 51). This is an exceptionally important consideration, and one that is deepened greatly by John Paul II in TOB. Wojtyla stresses that "existence is the first and basic good for every creature," and that the sexual urge in man has an "existential significance, for it is closely bound up with the whole existence of the species *Homo*" (p. 52). But *Homo sapiens* is a species unique among bodily living creatures. Why? Because unlike them it designates a species all of whose members are *persons* made in the image and likeness of God and called to life eternal with him. Hence the sexual urge orienting us toward the existence of the species *man* as its proper end is something deeply *personal*. This is most significant. Wojtyla does not regard the procreative meaning of human sexuality as something merely biological; rather it *is* personal, for it is this meaning of human sexuality that is oriented to the preservation of the species, to the prolongation of persons:

> But if the sexual urge has an existential character, if it is bound up with the very existence of the human person — that first and most basic good — then it must be subject to the principles which are binding in respect of the person. Hence, although the sexual urge is there for man to use, it must never be used in the absence of, or worse still, in a way which contradicts, love for the person. (p. 52)

It therefore follows that deliberate attempts to impede the existential (procreative) significance of the sexual urge will have a damaging effect upon love between persons (p. 53). The bond between the sexual urge and the existence of human persons "gives the sexual urge its objective importance and meaning" (p. 53). This is reflected in the character of true conjugal love of persons who "facilitate the existence of another concrete person, their own child, blood of their blood, and flesh of their flesh. This person is at once an affirmation and a continuation of their own love" (p. 53). When a man and a woman marry it is surely natural and not surprising that they have children, and the conception and birth of a child is the occasion for great joy that here at last is another person like ourselves, a new living image of God himself, a gift from God.

Pope John Paul II develops the ideas set forth here in TOB 20–22, where he analyzes the biblical meaning of "knowledge," human procreation, motherhood, and fatherhood, and again in TOB 118–125, where he defends the teaching of *Humanae Vitae.*

Love and Responsibility, Chapter 2: The Person and Love

Chapter 2 is rich in content and wide in scope; it is also difficult for ordinary readers. In it Wojtyla provides "metaphysical, psychological, and ethical" analyses of love. I will focus on these ideas and themes:

1. love as attraction, desire, good will, friendship;
2. "betrothed" or spousal love;
3. sensuality and sentiment or affection as "raw material for love" and the problem of integrating these materials into authentic love; and

4. the ethical analysis of love: love as a virtue and the personalistic norm.

1. Love as Attraction, Desire, Goodwill, Friendship

Put simply, love as *attraction* here means that a man, for instance, is attracted to a woman and vice versa, not merely because of sexual values but as a person of the opposite sex. Love as *desire* is, as it were, a "need love": a person is in need of something — here "some one" — in order to fulfill or complete himself. It is not necessarily selfish but can become so; it is essentially a basic human kind of love, a love for what is fulfilling. Love as *goodwill* seems pretty clear. One person wills that others flourish, that the goods of human existence flourish in them, and is unwilling deliberately to deprive them of these goods. Love of *friendship* also seems obvious. It is love that is reciprocated, and it is a love that loves that other person as "another self," as one for whom one is willing to sacrifice oneself, for example. It is a noble kind of love.

I will now present Wojtyla's analysis of these forms of love: As *attraction* love includes a cognitive element, but in attraction there is also a commitment of the will. Moreover, because the human person is a bodily being, attraction involves the emotions but goes beyond them to focus on the person who is the source of the attraction. Wojtyla stresses that attraction is of the essence of love and is in some way love itself, "*although love is not merely attraction*" (p. 76). Attraction is "one of the essential aspects of love as a whole" (pp. 76–77). One is attracted to a value one finds in a person, a value to which one is particularly sensitive. But love as attraction must be rooted in the *truth*; emotional-affective reactions, in which the object is *not* the truth, can distort or falsify attractions — if so, emotional love easily turns to hate, as we know too painfully from experience (see pp. 77–78). Thus in any attraction "the question of the truth about the person towards whom it is felt is so important ... [that] the truth about the person who is its object must play a part at least as important as the truth of the sentiments" (p. 78) — and obviously sexual values can elicit attraction. It is therefore important, Wojtyla continues, that there is a direct attraction to the person: "response to particular qualities inherent in a person must go with a simultaneous response to the qualities of the person as such, an awareness that a person as such is a value, and not merely attractive because of certain qualities which he or she possesses" (p. 79).

Desire belongs to the very essence of love, because the human person, as a limited and not self-sufficient being, is in *need* of other beings (p. 80). In particular, a man as a being of the male sex is in need of a woman as a being of the female sex and vice versa: the two are "complementary," i.e., they help fulfill each other, and the sexual urge is oriented in part to this completion of the one sex by the other. "This is 'love as desire,' for it originates in a need and aims at finding a good which it lacks. For a man, that good is a woman, for a woman it is a man" (p. 81). This truth is rooted, I note here, in Scripture, for after creating Adam the Lord God said: "It is not good for the man to be alone. I will make a suitable partner for him" (Gen 2:18).

But "there is ... a profound difference between love as desire (*amor concupiscentia*) and desire itself (*concupiscentia*), especially sensual desire." Desire as such implies a utilitarian attitude. Hence

> love as desire cannot then be reduced to desire itself. It is simply the crystallization of the objective need of one being directed towards another being which is for it a good and

an object of longing. *In the mind of the subject love-as-desire is not felt as mere desire. It is felt as a longing for some good for its own sake.... [L]ove is therefore apprehended as a longing for the person, and not as mere sensual desire, concupiscentia.* Desire goes together with this longing, but is so to speak overshadowed by it. (p. 81; emphasis added)

In TOB Pope John Paul develops what is said here about love as attraction and desire. There he is at pains to show that *eros* — the attraction to what is good — must not be confused with concupiscent desire and that it is not opposed to *ethos*. To put it another way, there is no contradiction between love as *eros* and ethical values, specifically the incomparable value of the human person. Indeed, he emphasizes that "The call to what is true, good, and beautiful [= eros] means ... the necessity of overcoming what derives from the threefold concupiscence" (47.5). He develops this further in TOB 49–50 when considering fallen man, who is subject to concupiscent desire, in the perspective of the resurrection won by Christ.

Love as goodwill or benevolence must also be recognized. This is essential to love between persons. It is unselfish love, for goodwill is free of self-interest and is indeed "*selflessness* in love.... Love as goodwill, *amor benevolentiae*, is therefore love in a more unconditional sense than love-desire" (p. 83). This is the self-giving love of which the ultimate source is God himself, whose son Jesus enables us to love even as we are loved by God in him.

Love as friendship, one special kind of which characterizes the love between husband and wife, is a love that exists *between* them, suggesting that "love is not just something *in* the man and something *in* the woman ... but is something common to them and unique" (p. 84). But how is it possible for persons, who are as such incommunicable, to enter into communion? How can the "I" and the "thou" become a "we"? The answer is found in the will, in the fact that we can freely choose to give ourselves to another in a love of friendship. "The fact is that a person who desires another as a good desires above all that person's love in return for his or her own love, desires that is to say another person above all as co-creator of love" (pp. 85–86). Love of friendship demands a full commitment of one's will to another person with a view to that person's good (p. 92). Love between man and woman, especially between husband and wife, must be rooted in friendship.

2. "Betrothed" or Spousal Love

This unique kind of friendship love, the kind of love that unites husband and wife, is possible because human persons can freely choose to give themselves completely to one another. The essence of this love is "self-giving, the surrender of one's 'I'" (p. 96). This is an interpersonal love that is deeper than friendship. "Betrothed love" in *Love and Responsibility* is what John Paul II calls "spousal love" in the TOB. I have already noted this and given relevant references to specific catecheses.

I have also already noted that in "giving" themselves to one another in marriage and in "receiving" one another as husband and wife, a man and a woman commit themselves irrevocably to each other and to marriage, an intimate partnership or covenant of life and love, and to the "goods" of marriage: faithful spousal love, children, and the effort to help each other become saints.

A paradox is involved here, for persons are incommunicable, in the sense that I am I and you are you. I am one person, my wife is a completely different person, and I can never *be* her or she me. Yet in betrothed love there is a full communication of persons, what Wojtyla later will term a *communio personarum* — a full surrendering of the self to another without losing possession of the self. What is paradoxical is that "in giving ourselves we find clear proof that we possess ourselves" (p. 98). "The concept of betrothed love implies the giving of the individual person to another chosen person" (p. 98). Marriage is rooted in betrothed love, which satisfies the demands of the personalistic norm. What Wojtyla calls "betrothed" love in *Love and Responsibility* is the same as what is meant by "conjugal" or "nuptial" love. It is the specific kind of love meant to exist between spouses, the kind of love that leads them to sacrifice themselves willingly for each other and for the "common good" of marriage, to which they had freely committed themselves. "This giving of oneself ... cannot, in marriage or indeed in any relationship between persons of opposite sex, have a merely sexual significance. Giving oneself only sexually, without the full gift of the person to validate it, must lead to ... utilitarianism.... A personalistic interpretation is ... absolutely necessary." Marriage is the "result of this form of love" (p. 99).

3. Sensuality and Sentiment or Affectivity as "Raw Material for Love" and Their Integration

Sensuality is rooted in the truth that because men and women are bodily, sexual beings, they naturally impress one another as persons of this kind and elicit a response. Among the responses is sensuality, a response to the sexual values of the body-person and a response to the person as a "potential object of enjoyment." Thus sensuality has a "consumer orientation," being directed "primarily and immediately towards a 'body,'" and touching the person only "indirectly." Because sensuality is directed to using the body as an object, it even interferes with the apprehension of the body as beautiful — as an object of contemplative cognition and of enjoyment in that Augustinian meaning of the term (p. 105).

But it is important to recognize that "this [consumer] orientation of sensuality is a matter of spontaneous reflexes," and is not "primarily an evil thing but a natural thing" (p. 106):

> Sensuality expresses itself mainly in an appetitive form: a person of the other sex is seen as an "object of desire" specifically because of the sexual value inherent in the body itself, for it is in the body that the senses discover that which determines sexual difference, sexual "otherness." (p. 107)

All of us have experienced sensuality in our lives. This is the reason why men, for example, like to watch pretty women pass on the street. But the human person, Wojtyla goes on to say,

> cannot be an object for use. Now, the body is an integral part of the person, and so must not be treated as though it were detached from the whole person: both the value of the body and the sexual value which finds expression in the body depend upon the value of the person.... [A] sensual reaction in which the body and sex are a possible object for use threatens to devalue the person. (p. 107)

Thus sensuality, although not evil in itself, poses a threat and a temptation. It is, however, "a sort of raw material for true, conjugal love." But since it is "blind to the person, and oriented only towards the sexual value connected with 'the body,'" it is "fickle, turning wherever it finds that value, wherever a 'possible object of enjoyment' appears" (p. 108). How true! But this natural response of the person to the sexual values of the body of a person of the opposite sex is not in itself morally wrong. In fact, Wojtyla declares: "an exuberant and readily roused sensuality is the stuff from which a rich — if difficult — personal life may be made" (p. 109). Sensuality, in short, is a natural emotional response to the sexual values of the body of a person of the opposite sex. To reject it is foolish and unnatural. But we must not allow this natural response to degenerate into lustful concupiscence, and at times this can be difficult.

Sentimentality (= affectivity), another deeply felt response to the body-person, differs from sensuality because it is oriented "to the sexual value residing in 'a whole person of the other sex,' to 'femininity' or 'masculinity'" (p. 110). It is the source of affection. While based, as is sensuality, on a sensory intuition, its content is

> the whole "person of the other sex," the whole "woman" or "man." For sensuality, one part of this integral sense impression "the body" immediately stands out from and is as it were dissociated from the rest [namely, the "sexual value"], whereas sentiment remains attached to a whole individual of the other sex. (p. 110)

Thus affection seems free of the concupiscence of which sensuality is full. But a different kind of desire is present, a "desire for nearness, for proximity ... for exclusivity or intimacy" (p. 110). This leads to tenderness and, unfortunately, can easily shift into the territory of sensuality, this time a sensuality disguised as sentiment (p. 111). It gives rise to "sentimental love" or what we would call romantic or puppy love, in which one person becomes infatuated with another. The problem here is that this can give rise to an idealization of the object of love — one idealizes the object of sentimental love because one wants that object to be the one who gives the subjective feeling of intimacy, and so forth. Although "raw material" for love, sentiment is *not* love because it is blind to the *person* and fixed on the subjective feelings that the idealized person can give. Thus:

> [I]f "love" remains just sensuality, just a matter of "sex appeal," it will not be love at all, but only the utilization of one person by another, or of two persons by each other. While if love remains mere sentiment it will equally be unlike love in the complete sense of the word. For both persons will remain in spite of everything divided from each other, though it may appear that they are very close just because they so eagerly seek proximity.... (pp. 113–114)

The point is that the proximity is not sought because one loves the *person* but rather because one loves the subjective feeling of affection the idealized person communicates.

Sensuality and sentiment can be integrated into true interpersonal love, especially between man and woman, only in the light of truth and only by free, self-determining choice: *"The process of integrating love relies on the primary elements of the human spirit — freedom and truth"* (p. 116). Because we are persons, we are not compelled to act on the basis of emotional responses. As persons, we can deliberate about what we are to do and freely choose to do this or that. Moreover, we know that we are never to "use" persons merely as means to gratify our desires or emotions. We can thus appreciate the sexual values of a person of the opposite sex without seeking to "consume" those values as a commodity, and we can recognize a person of the other sex as one who in some ways "embodies" femininity or masculinity without becoming infatuated, making fools of ourselves ("infatuate" comes from the Latin word *fatus*, which means "fool"). As we will see, what enables us to "integrate" sensuality and sentiment into authentic love is the virtue of chastity.

In TOB 100.129, in offering a sketch of "conjugal spirituality," Pope John Paul II writes beautifully of the role that the virtue of chastity, by means of conjugal continence (integral to but not the whole of chastity), plays in mediating between what he there calls "arousal," which is bodily in character and focuses on the sexual values of the other, and "emotion," which focuses on the "wholeness" of the person of the other. For example, a husband is naturally aroused on seeing his wife naked (sensuality is operative here), but he is also attracted to her as embodying "femininity." He is in some way "smitten" by her. But these feelings have been integrated in him by means of conjugal continence, whereby he realizes that these feelings must be subordinated to and in accord with reason, with the truth that she, like himself, is a person to whom the only adequate response is love. This "mediation" enables spouses, he then says, "to direct sensual and emotive reactions in order to allow the *gift* of self to the other 'I' *on the basis of the* mature *possession* of one's own 'I' in its bodily and emotive subjectivity" (130.4). I consider this a new development of this section of *Love and Responsibility*, in which he identifies sensuality and sentiment or affectivity as "raw materials" of love that must be integrated, as he goes on to show in chapter 3, into the person through the virtue of chastity.

4. The Ethical Analysis of Love

Wojtyla insists that it is impossible to integrate the various elements of love, to have psychological completeness in love, unless ethical completeness is attained (p. 120). This is possible only by considering love as a virtue acquired when one shapes one's choices in the light of the truth, in particular the truth of the personalistic norm.

This first requires affirmation of the value of the person, and attraction to the sexual values of the person must be subordinated to a reverence for the incalculable dignity of the person. Love "is directed not towards 'the body' alone, nor yet towards 'a human being of the other sex,' but precisely towards a person. What is more, it is only when it directs itself [through free choice] to the person that love is love" (p. 123). This leads to the "self-giving" characteristic of "betrothed love," a love based on reciprocity and friendship, and rooted in commitment to a common, shared good (pp. 126–127). Sexual relations are in accord with the personalistic norm only when they take place between persons who are already completely united in this kind of love (i.e., in marriage). Before the love of a man and woman can

> take on its definitive form, become "betrothed love," the man and the woman each face the choice of the person on whom to bestow the gift of self.... The object of choice is another person, but it is as though one were choosing another "I," choosing oneself in another, and the other in oneself. Only if it is objectively good for two persons to be together can they belong to each other. (p. 131)

These ideas are richly developed in TOB in catecheses devoted to the spousal meaning of the body, both in the state of original innocence and afterward when one has "recovered" this meaning by participation in the redemptive death of Christ. See chapter 3 of this book, "John Paul II's Catecheses on the Theology of the Body" below.

Love and Responsibility, Chapter 3: The Person and Chastity

The purpose of chapter 3 is to show that the virtue of chastity, far from being something negative, is something very positive. It is, in fact, the virtue that enables us to come into possession of our sexual desires and emotions, in particular our sensuality and sentiment. Those are what Wojtyla had described as the "raw material of love," allowing us to give ourselves away in love to others. He finds it necessary first to "rehabilitate" chastity insofar as in the contemporary world it has acquired a negative meaning. He then makes important distinctions between concupiscence, carnal desire, and sinful love before developing the real meaning of chastity. He concludes with a magnificent discussion of what he calls the "metaphysics of shame" and the difference between continence and chastity.

In this section, I will focus on three themes that I consider especially important in relation to the theology of the body.

1. the "rehabilitation" of chastity;
2. concupiscence, carnal desire, and sinful love;
3. the true meaning of chastity.

1. The "Rehabilitation" of Chastity

Today there is hostile resentment even to talk about chastity because of a distorted sense of values as well as from human laziness. In the face of this hostile environment, it is necessary to "rehabilitate" chastity. In our culture it is basically assumed that contraception is a normal, natural way to cope with difficult problems, and that those who think that it is immoral are simply "not with it." It is thus necessary to rehabilitate the reasons why contraception is always wrong and to teach that there are much better ways to cope with the situations for which it is invoked as a panacea. The same is true of the virtue of chastity. But chastity, far from being hostile to love, in fact enables us to love rightly, for it frees us from "everything that 'makes dirty'" and is rooted in an "attitude to a person of the opposite sex which derives from sincere affirmation of the worth of that person" (p. 146).

2. Concupiscence, Carnal Desire, and Sinful Love

To understand the function of chastity we need first to consider the issue of concupiscence, carnal desire, and "sinful" love. We have already seen how sensuality and sentiment or affectivity provide "raw material for love" but become love only when raised to the personal level, by reciprocal affirmation of the value of the person. But human persons are subject, as a result of original sin, to concupiscence, "a consistent tendency to see persons of the other sex through the prism of sexuality alone, as 'objects of potential enjoyment.'" But "the correct way to see and 'desire' a person is through the medium of his or her value as a person. We should not think of this manner of seeing and desiring as 'asexual,' as blind to the value of the 'body and sex; ... it is simply that this value must be correctly integrated with love of the person ... *[H]ence the distinction between 'love of the body'* [which is good] *and 'carnal love'* [which is not]" (pp. 159–160). The problem is that sensuality and sentiment can be "swallowed up by concupiscence" and not absorbed by true love.

Neither sensuality nor carnal desire is itself a sin (Catholic theology sees in concupiscence, which results from original sin, not sin as such, but the "germ" of sin). Sin enters in only when the will "consents." Authentic love, which absorbs sensuality and sentiment, must be clearly distinguished from "sinful love." This love

> is often very emotional, saturated in emotion, which leaves no room for anything else. Its sinfulness is not of course due to the fact that it is saturated with emotion, nor to the emotion itself, but to the fact that the will puts emotion before the person, allowing it to annul all the objective laws and principles which must govern the unification of two persons, a man and a woman.

Wojtyla goes on to say, in a most perceptive passage: *"'Authenticity' of feeling is quite often inimical to truth in behavior"* (p. 163). The result is that one is led to the false judgment that "what is pleasant is good." Moreover:

> [T]he particular danger of "sinful love" consists in a fiction: immediately, and before reflection, it is not felt to be "sinful," but it is, above all, felt to be love. The direct effect of this circumstance, it is true, is to reduce the gravity of the sin, but indirectly it makes the sin more dangerous. The fact that very many "acts" in the association and cohabitation of man and woman occur spontaneously, under the influence of emotion, does not in the least alter the fact that the personalistic norm exists and is also binding in relations between persons. Only on the basis of the principle embodied in it can we speak of the unification of two persons in love, *and this is equally true of married love* [emphasis added], in which the union of man and woman is complemented by sexual partnership (p. 165).... We can see then that the sin in "sinful love" is essentially rooted in free will. Carnal desire is only its germ. For the will can and must prevent the "dis-integration" of love — prevent pleasure, or indeed emotion from growing to the dimensions of goods in their own right, while all else in the relationship of two persons of different sexes is subordinate to them. The will can and must be guided by objective truth. (p. 166)

3. *The True Meaning of Chastity*

In the Catholic tradition rooted in Scripture (cf. e.g., 1 Cor 6), the Fathers and Doctors of the Church, in particular Saint Thomas Aquinas, considered chastity as an integral part of the cardinal virtue of temperance. This was also true, in a way, in the Aristotelian philosophical tradition. This tradition had recognized four "cardinal" virtues (so called because other virtues "hinged" — from the Latin word *cardo* meaning hinge — on them): prudence (perfecting the practical intellect), justice (perfecting the will), fortitude (perfecting the "irascible" appetite), and temperance (perfecting the "concupiscible" appetite). In this schema chastity is linked to the cardinal virtue of temperance or moderation. Temperance helps us to control our desires, especially regarding food and sex. This virtue helps us to be more fully human by regulating our desires through the use of reason. As Wojtyla says, temperance

> restrain[s] the instinctive appetites for various material and bodily goods which force themselves upon the senses. Sensual reactions ... must be subordinated to reason: this is the function of the virtue of moderation.... It is natural, that is in accordance with nature, for a reasonable being such as man is to desire and strive for that which reason recognizes as good. (p. 168)

Wojtyla describes the function of the virtue of chastity in this framework by stressing that it (chastity) is "simply a matter of efficiency in controlling the concupiscent impulses." This means constant effectiveness: "Fully formed virtue is an efficiently functioning control which permanently keeps the appetites in equilibrium by means of its habitual attitude to the true good (*bonum honestum*) determined by reason" (p. 169). But, and this is the crucial meaning of chastity: "*Chastity can only be thought of in association with the virtue of love*," and its "function is to free love from the utilitarian attitude" (p. 169).

> The virtue of chastity, whose function it is to free love from utilitarian attitudes, must control not only sensuality and carnal concupiscence, as such, but — perhaps more important — those centers deep within the human being in which the util-

itarian attitude is hatched and grows. There can be no chastity unless the forms of volitional subjectivism of which I have spoken, and the varieties of egoism which they conceal, are overcome: *the more successfully the utilitarian attitude is camouflaged in the will the more dangerous it is....* To be chaste means to have a "transparent" attitude to a person of the other sex — *chastity means just that* — *the interior "transparency"* without which love is not itself, for it cannot be itself until the desire to "enjoy" is subordinated to a readiness to show loving kindness in every situation. (p. 170)

This does not mean that chastity is negative; it is rather positive, a yes to the value of the human person, a yes to raising all reactions to the value of "the body and sex" to the level of the person (pp. 170–171). I think I could sum Wojtyla up by saying that chastity is the virtue enabling a person to come into possession of his sexual desires and feelings, not to be possessed by them, so that he can give himself away in love to others, particularly to persons of the other sex.

TOB 24–63, in which John Paul II offers his analyses of Jesus' teaching in the Sermon on the Mount and his reflections on our ability, in and with Christ, to overcome concupiscent desire, and of Saint Paul's teaching on purity of heart, develop these ideas, as already noted. In addition, he offers even further development in his outline of conjugal spirituality in TOB 126–132.

Love and Responsibility, Chapter 4: Justice Toward the Creator

The central themes of this chapter are:

1. marriage: monogamous and indissoluble;
2. the value of marriage as an institution;

3. marriage and family;
4. procreation and parenthood;
5. periodic continence;
6. marital intercourse and "justice to God the Creator";
7. vocation, virginity, marriage, and parenthood.

1. Marriage: Monogamous and Indissoluble

The personalistic norm demands that marriage be monogamous and indissoluble because only in this way is the dignity of the person fully respected. Other arrangements fall short of this norm's strict demands by putting "one person in the position of an object to be enjoyed by another" (p. 211). This demand of the personalistic norm, which binds once marriage has come into existence despite subsequent desires on the part of husband or wife, is rooted in two important truths: (1) human choices, made in the light of the truth (see p. 214) *determine* the self, and (2) in choosing to marry, a man and woman freely give themselves the identity of husband and wife, committing themselves henceforth to be utterly faithful to one another.

2. The Value of the Institution of Marriage

The "institution of marriage" justifies the intimate sexual relationship between husband and wife in the eyes of society. The value of marriage as an institution is that *it serves to protect conjugal love* or the community of persons made one because of their love, and thereby "provides a justification for the sexual relationship between a particular couple within the whole complex of society" (p. 219). To put it somewhat differently, "In a society which accepts sound ethical principles and lives in accordance with them ... this institution is necessary to signify the maturity of the union between a man and a woman, to testify that theirs is a love on which a lasting union and community can be based" (p. 220).

3. Marriage and Family

Although distinct, marriage and family are intimately bound together. "The birth of a child turns the union of a man and a woman based on the sexual relationship into a family," which is itself "the primary institution at the base of our existence as human beings." The distinct existence, character, and ends of the family must therefore be protected by legislation. For a society to legislate justly regarding the family, it must recognize the rights and duties of marriage, acknowledging that "the family is an institution based on marriage" (p. 217). Marriage must not be regarded merely as a means instrumental to the founding of a family, but must be recognized as something good in itself: "The inner and essential *raison d'etre* of marriage is not simply eventual transformation into a family but above all the creation of a lasting personal union between a man and a woman based on love. Marriage serves above all to preserve the existence of the species ... but it is based on love" (p. 218).

4. Procreation and Parenthood

Marriage is a "state," a durable institution providing the framework necessary to justify the existence of sexual relations between a man and a woman. Moreover, within marriage sexual relations are ongoing, with a regular succession of acts. But every such act within marriage must have its own internal justification and meet the objective demands of the personalistic norm: "It is in this context more than in any other that people must show responsibility for their love. Let us add at once that this responsibility for love is complemented by responsibility for life and health: a combination of fundamental goods which together determine the moral value of every marital act" (p. 225). One condition for the realization of love is a correct attitude toward procreation.

> When a man and a woman consciously and of their own free will choose to marry and have sexual relations, they choose at the same time the possibility of procreation, *choose to participate in creation* (for that is the proper meaning of the word procreation). And it is only when they do so that they put their sexual relationship within the framework of marriage on a truly personal level. (p. 227)

The marital union must

> be accompanied by awareness and *willing acceptance* of the possibility that "I may become a father" or "I may become a mother." Without this the marital relationship will not be "internally" justified ... the union of persons is not the same as sexual union. This latter is raised to the level of the person only when it is accompanied in the mind and the will by the acceptance of the possibility of parenthood. (pp. 227–228; emphasis added)

The deliberate attempt to prevent conception by artificial means entails a refusal to accept this possibility; thus artificial contraception is immoral and violates the personalistic norm. Consequently, the only solution to the problem regarding the legitimate regulation of birth within marriage is continence, which demands control over erotic experiences. When a man and a woman who have marital intercourse "decisively preclude the possibility of paternity and maternity, their intentions are thereby diverted from the person and directed to mere enjoyment.... By definitively precluding the possibility of procreation in the marital act a man and a woman inevitably shift the whole focus of the experience in the direction of sexual pleasure as such" (pp. 234–235).

5. *Periodic Continence*

Periodic continence is the only way to face the problem of birth regulation, because continence is a "condition of love, the only attitude towards a partner in marriage, and particularly towards a wife, compatible with affirmation of the value of the person" (p. 237). If husband and wife have good reasons to avoid a pregnancy, they must remain continent and abstain from the act that could cause the pregnancy. "Those who do not desire the consequence [conception of a child after freely chosen sex] must avoid the cause" (p. 239). But if spouses limit intercourse to infertile times, how can they say that they are engaging in intercourse with a willingness to become parents? This question demands the right interpretation of periodic continence. This entails understanding that it is licit because it does not conflict with the personalistic norm. Periodic continence does not deliberately close the conjugal act to the gift of life. Above all, such continence means that "in the wills of the persons concerned it must be grounded in a sufficiently mature virtue" (p. 241), and "*is permissible only in so far as it does not conflict with a sincere disposition to procreate*" (p. 243).

6. *Marital Intercourse and "Justice to God the Creator"*

Marital relations must be justified not only "horizontally," i.e., in the eyes of society, but also and more so "vertically," giving justice to God the Creator. Our obligations toward the Creator come under the virtue of religion, which Saint Thomas identified as a potential part of justice. It is potential because justice in the strict sense cannot be given to God— we can never render to him perfectly all that is due to him.

But elementary justice toward God, demanded by the virtue of religion, requires the "*understanding and rational acceptance of the order of nature*," which is at one and the same time "*recognition of the rights of the Creator*" (p. 246).

This is based on the truth that man can *understand* the order of nature and conform to it in his actions by freely choosing to respect fully the goods of human existence. Man, in short, "has a share in the law which God bestowed on the world when he created it at the beginning of time" (p. 246), and his intelligent participation in this law enables him to be a cooperator with God. Because husband and wife are persons, "they take part consciously in the work of creation (*pro-creatio*), and from this point of view are *participes Creatoris*." Precisely for this reason "the question of justice towards the Creator arises both in married life and in any form of relationship or association between people of different sexes." Precisely because the person transcends the world of nature, "a man and a woman who have marital relations fulfill their obligations to God the Creator only when they raise their relationship to the level of love, to the level of a truly personal union" (pp. 248–249).

Justice to the Creator means that "I must offer him all that is in me, my whole being, for he has first claim on all of it." Since it is impossible to give God all that is due him, we cannot render him complete justice. But Christ has offered us a solution—love. "*Self-giving has other roots—not justice, but love*" (p. 250); moreover, love does something that justice cannot do: it unites persons.

7. Vocation, Virginity, Marriage, and Parenthood

Only persons have vocations. The term "vocation" indicates that "*there is a proper course for every person's development to follow*, a specific way in which he commits his whole life to the service of certain values" (p. 256). Moreover, each one's vocation requires that he or she fix his or her love on some goal, love someone, and be prepared to give himself or herself for love. Vocation, in short, demands self-giving. Sincere self-giving is central to both marriage and virginity understood as the full gift of oneself to God, understood, in short, in a personalistic way. In the vision of the New Testament each of us is summoned to give himself fully in love to God and others. Moreover, as this vision makes clear, we cannot do this relying only on our own interior resources. "In calling upon us to seek perfection, the Gospel also requires us to believe in divine Grace"—to rely on God's help (pp. 257–258). All of us have the vocation to holiness, to perfection.

In light of the union of love between God and man, the idea of virginity acquires full significance. Literally, it means "untouched," and its physical sign is that one is untouched from the sexual point of view. "Physical virginity is an external expression of the fact that the person belongs only to itself and to the Creator." In marriage the woman "surrenders" her virginity to her husband and ceases to be a virgin in the physical sense, while the husband ceases to be a virgin by coming into "possession" of his wife. All this, however, is understood as a relationship rooted in reciprocal, betrothed love (p. 251).

"Within man's relationship with God, understood as a relationship of love, *man's posture can and must be one of surrender to God*" (p. 251; emphasis added). This means that the relationship of man, male and female, as creature to God the Creator, is analogous to the relationship of female to male: the creature "surrenders" his or her virginity to God the Creator— the uncreated Spouse. This opens up the "possibility of betrothed and requited love between God and man: the human soul, which is the betrothed of God, gives itself to him alone ... under the influence of Grace" (p. 251).

This is the core meaning of "mystical" or "spiritual" virginity, which is not only possible but also essential for married men and women. It is true that we do not speak of virginity in the case of married persons who give themselves wholly to God, "although giving oneself to God as an act of betrothed love may be analogous to that which constitutes the essence of virginity" (p. 252).

"Man has an inborn need of betrothed love, a need to give himself to another" (p. 253). Christ and the Church recognize virginity (physical and spiritual) as a choice for God—for being betrothed to him: "The man who chooses virginity chooses God" (p. 253).

> This does not, however, mean that in choosing marriage he renounces God for a human being. Marriage and the betrothed love for a human being which goes with it, the dedication of oneself to another person, solves the problem of the union of persons only on the terrestrial and temporal scale. The union of person with person here takes place in the physical and sexual sense, in accordance with man's physical nature and the natural effects of the sexual urge. *Nevertheless, the need to give oneself to another person has profounder origins than the sexual instinct, and is connected above all with the spiritual nature of the human person. It is not sexuality which creates in a man and a woman the need to give themselves to each other but, on the contrary, it is the need to give oneself, latent in every human person, which finds its outlet in the conditions of existence in the body, and on the basis of the sexual urge, in physical and sexual union, in matrimony. But the need for betrothed love, the need to give oneself to and unite with another person, is deeper and connected with the spiritual existence of the person.*(p. 253; emphasis added)

Parenthood, whether fatherhood or motherhood, is rooted in the inner life; it is a new way of crystallizing a husband's love for his wife, and a wife's love for her husband. Motherhood or maternity seems more "natural," i.e., tied to the nature of the female organism, than fatherhood or paternity. Paternity or fatherhood is thus more a result of culture than of nature. Paternity and maternity are deeper than biology and are spiritual in nature: we beget our children in the spirit, and the model parent here is God the Father.

Love and Responsibility, Chapter 5: Sexology and Ethics

Two topics presented in this chapter are of most significance for us in relation to TOB. These are:

1. marriage and marital intercourse;
2. the problem of birth control.

Before summarizing this matter, it is useful to note Wojtyla's introductory remarks. He emphasizes the superiority of ethics (a normative science) over empirical studies, and he repudiates what he calls "pure sexology," i.e., an attempt to deal with problems of sexual life from a purely medical or physiological point of view (as with Kinsey, Masters and Johnson, et al.). Since man is a person, ethics and love take precedence over physiology. However, if the sexologist acknowledges that the sexual beings he studies are persons to whom the only adequate response is love, his knowledge can contribute to sexual ethics. Such an ethics-based sexology is a legitimate branch of the science and art of medicine, whose proper concern is care of health and preservation of life. Nonetheless, good medicine (and thus good clinical sexology) realizes that the subject of life and health is a person, and that, with respect to sexual life and the relationship between the sexes, "*What matters is the man's duty to the woman, and the woman's duty to the man by virtue of the fact that they are both persons, and not merely what is beneficial to their health*" (p. 266).

1. Marriage and Marital Intercourse

Males must become aware of the very different way in which sexual excitement reaches its climax in females than in males, as Wojtyla notes. "From the point of view of another person, from the altruistic standpoint, it is necessary to insist that intercourse must not serve merely as a means of allowing sexual excitement to reach its climax in one of the partners, i.e. the man alone, but that climax must be reached in harmony, not at the expense of one partner, but with both partners fully involved" (p. 272). In short, husbands ought to learn how to please their wives by becoming familiar with the findings of sexology in this matter. "Non-observance of these teachings of sexology in the marital relationship is contrary to the good of the other partner to the marriage and the durability and cohesion of the marriage itself" (p. 273). If insufficient heed is paid to such truths, the wife, who will not be fully involved, may begin to have a hostile attitude toward sex, become frigid in some way, and even experience psychological and physiological damage (see p. 273).

It is not good for the wife to pretend to have a "sham orgasm," because this conceals the problem and can at best be a palliative. Wojtyla pleads for true personal education in the matter and distinguishes between a "culture of marital relations" and concern for mere technique—the "how to" manual approach (see pp. 274–275). What is most needed is true love. Finally, the valid findings of sexology, while not directly supporting monogamy and indissolubility, nonetheless do so indirectly because of the importance of these findings to the psychological and physical health of spouses, and this health flourishes best in the soil of true marital love (see pp. 276–277).

2. The Problem of Birth Control

Wojtyla develops ideas set forth in chapter 4 on this topic. Before getting to the moral problem he briefly (see pp. 279–281) discusses the nature of the woman's fertile cycle. In these pages he indicates that fear of conception (at a time when it would not be appropriate for the wife to become pregnant) is perhaps the most common psychological factor upsetting the woman's natural cycle (and making periodic continence more difficult). The proper moral stance regarding birth control can be reduced to two elements: "readiness during intercourse to accept parenthood … and that readiness to practice continence which derives from virtue, from love for the closest of persons" (p. 281).

Wojtyla notes how chemical and mechanical means can cause harm to the woman's health and how coitus interruptus is both ineffective and robs the woman of orgasm. The only morally correct method is the natural means of control (which is not contraceptive), used not as a mere technique but as an exercise of the virtue of continence. He stresses that

> a more important task for the man than adapting himself to the biological cycle of the woman is the creation of a favorable psychological climate for their relationship without which the successful application of natural methods is out of the question. This demands the regular practice of continence on the part of the man, so that birth control by natural means depends in the last analysis on the moral attitude of the male.

The marital relationship demands on his part tenderness, an understanding for the feelings of the woman. (pp. 283–284)

As we will see in chapter 3, John Paul II magnificently develops this teaching on contraception and the practice of periodic continence in his catecheses on TOB.

Familiaris Consortio (The Role of the Christian Family in the Modern World) and the Theology of the Body

The great document *Familiaris Consortio*, published on November 22, 1981, was issued in response to the Fifth Ordinary General Synod of Bishops devoted to the Christian family that met at the end of September and beginning of October 1980. To prepare for this important meeting, Pope John Paul II had begun, on September 5, 1979, his audiences on TOB. By the time the synod met he had given forty-one of those addresses, and by November 1981 some sixty-three of the addresses, approximately half of the total, had been delivered. Thus *Familiaris Consortio* includes many of the fundamental ideas and themes of TOB.

In presenting *this magisterial document* to the public, John Paul II described it as a "*summa* of the teaching of the Church on the life, the tasks, the responsibilities, and the mission of marriage and the family in the world today."

The exhortation is divided into the following parts:

Introduction (nos. 1–3)
PART I: Bright Spots and Shadows for the Family Today
(4–10)

PART 2: The Plan of God for Marriage and the Family (11–16)

PART 3: The Role of the Christian Family (17–64)

PART 4: Pastoral Care of the Family: Stages, Structures, Agents, and Situations (65–85)

Conclusion (86)

Since TOB is not in my judgment relevant to parts 1 and 4 of this great apostolic exhortation, I will not consider those parts here. But TOB is crucially important for and relevant to parts 2 and 3. Part 3 is by far the longest part of the document and richest with respect to TOB.

Familiaris Consortio, Part 2: The Plan of God for Marriage and the Family (11–16)

Part 2 of *Familiaris Consortio* is exceptionally powerful, brimming with themes and ideas central to TOB such as the dignity of human persons who are bodily and sexual beings called to love and to give themselves to others in love. I will indicate those parts that are in some ways, however briefly, recapitulated in this rich part of the apostolic exhortation.

Self-giving Love (11–13)

John Paul emphasizes that *human persons*, who have a fundamental and innate vocation to love as God loves (11.1–2), are *bodily beings* (11.3). Their "sexuality, by means of which man and woman give themselves to one another through the acts that are proper and exclusive to spouses … concerns the innermost being of the human person as such" (11.5). He insists that "it [sexuality] is realized in a truly human way only if it is an integral part of the love by which a man and a woman commit themselves totally to one another until death." So true is this that the self-giving "would be a lie if it were not the sign and fruit of a total personal self-giving, in which the whole person, including the temporal dimension, is present" (11.5). These themes and ideas recapitulate in brief form material developed in depth in TOB 1–23, in particular TOB 3–19, and 23, where John Paul considers the original unity of man and woman, the spousal meaning of the body, and marriage in an integral vision of man. They also recapitulate in a different way his teaching in chapter 2 of *Love and Responsibility* regarding the nature of "betrothed love" and the ethical analysis of love.

Service to Life (14)

Moreover, the end of the personal community vivified by love is service to life, to the good of procreation, to cooperating with God in giving life to new human persons:

> This totality [of giving] which is required by conjugal love also corresponds to the demands of responsible fertility. This fertility is directed to the generation of a human being, and so by its nature it surpasses the purely biological order and involves a whole series of personal values. (11.6)

All this is deepened in number 14, paragraphs 1 and 2, in which John Paul II insists, with *Gaudium et Spes*, that "the very institution of marriage and conjugal love are ordained to the procreation and education of children, in whom they find their crowning" (14.1). Children are indeed the crowning "gift" of marriage. This is beautifully illustrated by the joy and delight expressed by both mothers and fathers on beholding their infant child. He points out that

> love is essentially a gift, and conjugal love, while leading the spouses to the reciprocal "knowledge" which makes them

"one flesh," does not end with the couple, because it makes them capable of the greatest possible gift by which they become cooperators with God for giving life to a new human person. (14.2)

These themes and ideas are marvelously enriched in the catecheses found in TOB 20–22 that are devoted to "knowledge" and procreation and the dimensions of motherhood and fatherhood.

Marriage as a Sacrament (15)

Marriage is for Christians a sacrament, and its sacramentality deepens our understanding of the theology of the body. Because they are baptized Christians, spouses are "definitively placed within the new and eternal covenant, in the spousal covenant of Christ with the Church" (13.6). Christ crucified fully reveals God's love for us, and the marriage of Christians becomes a sign of and a participation in the New Covenant

> sanctioned in the blood of Christ. The Spirit which the Lord pours forth gives a new heart, and renders man and woman capable of loving one another as Christ has loved us. Conjugal love reaches that fullness to which it is interiorly ordered, conjugal charity, which is the proper and specific way in which the spouses participate in and are called to live the very charity of Christ who gave himself on the Cross. (13.3; cf. 13.6, 9; and 16.1, 5–6)

Indeed, as he says in 13.8:

> [Christian] spouses are therefore the permanent reminder to the Church of what happened on the cross ... [and] witnesses to the salvation in which the sacrament makes them sharers.... Of this salvation event marriage, like every sacrament, is a memorial, actuation and prophecy: "As a memorial, the sacrament gives them the grace and duty of commemorating

the great works of God and of bearing witness to them before their children. As actuation, it gives them the grace and duty of putting into practice in the present, towards each other and their children, the demands of a love which forgives and redeems. As prophecy, it gives them the grace and duty of living and bearing witness to the hope of the future encounter with Christ." [John Paul quoting an address he gave to the delegates of the Centre de Liaison des Equipes de Recherche (Nov. 3, 1979), 3: as found in *Insegnamenti di Giovanni Paolo II*, II, 2 (1979), 1038]

These are key themes magnificently developed in TOB 87–102, catecheses focused on John Paul II's analysis of Ephesians 5:21–28, where he considers marriage as a covenant of grace and love.

Virginity and Celibacy (16)

In part 2 of *Familiaris Consortio*, as in TOB 75–85, John Paul also emphasizes that virginity or celibacy undertaken for the sake of the kingdom, with marriage, is a vocation to love (11.4). Christians who freely choose virginity or celibacy for the sake of Christ's kingdom anticipate in a bodily way the eschatological marriage of Christ with his bride the Church (16.1, 3), and they also become spiritually fruitful, the father and mother of many, cooperating in the realization of the family according to God's plan (16.6). Again, these ideas are richly developed in TOB 75–85.

Familiaris Consortio, Part 3:
The Role of the Christian Family (17–64)

This lengthy part of *Familiaris Consortio* is subdivided into an introduction (17) and four major sections:

1. Forming a community of persons (18–27)
2. Serving life (28–41)
3. Participating in the development of society (42–48)
4. Sharing in the life and mission of the Church (49–64)

Of these sections the TOB catecheses bear directly on the first two and more indirectly on the final two.

In the introductory number to this part (17) John Paul II issues a challenge: "Family, become what you are!" This is a Pauline expression, for Saint Paul time and time again urged Christians to "become what they are." In and through Christ, by reason of God's initiative, they *are* saints, holy, new creatures, adopted sons of the Father, brothers of Christ and able to call his Father by the same name he did, "Abba!," a term of personal endearment. Their mission, their task as Christians, is to become fully what they are. And this is true of the Christian family. John Paul II clearly spells out what this means in the first two paragraphs of number 17:

> The family finds in the plan of God the Creator and Redeemer not only its *identity*, what it *is*, but also its *mission*, what it can and should *do*. *The role that God calls the family to perform in history derives from what the family is; its role represents the dynamic and existential development of what it is....* [Thus] *family become what you are.* (17.1; emphasis added)

Continuing, the Holy Father declares:

> Since in God's plan it has been established as an "intimate community of life and love" (*Gaudium et Spes*, 48), the family has the mission to become more and more what it is, that is to say, a community of life and love ... the essence and role of the family are ... specified by love. Hence the family has *the mission to guard, reveal and communicate love*, and this is a living reflection of and a real sharing in God's love for

humanity and the love of Christ the Lord for the Church his bride. (17.2)

Here we find echoes of what John Paul II has to say in TOB 1–23, where he offers catecheses on the original unity of man and woman in God's loving plan, the plan that, thanks to Christ's redemptive work, can and must be carried out in the world today by Christian families.

1. Forming a Community of Persons (18–27)

The family is a "community of persons: of husband and wife, of parents and children, of relatives," whose "first task is to live with fidelity the reality of communion in a constant effort to develop an authentic community of persons" (18.1). The inner principle of this task is love (18.2). This communion of persons begins with the communion of husband and wife. Their communion, rooted in their natural sexual complementarity (19.2), is purified and perfected by God through Christ, who in the sacrament of Matrimony gives husband and wife a "new heart," enabling them not only to overcome the "hardness of heart" but also, above all, to share the "full and definitive love of Christ, the new and eternal Covenant made flesh," who calls Christian couples "to participate truly in the irrevocable indissolubility that binds him to the Church his bride, loved by him to the end" (20.4).

This conjugal communion is the rock or foundation on which is built "the broader communion of the family, of parents and children, of brothers and sisters with each other, of relatives and other members of the household" (21.1). This communion is "rooted in the natural bonds of flesh and blood" (21.2), and is called "to experience a new and original communion [made possible by Christ's grace] which confirms and perfects natural and human communion," with the result that the "Christian family constitutes a specific revelation and realization of ecclesial communion, and for this reason too it can and should be called 'the domestic Church' (see *Lumen Gentium*, no. 11)" (21.3). Again all these ideas and themes echo deeply the catecheses of TOB noted already, in particular TOB 8–19, dealing with the meaning of original unity, nakedness without shame, and the spousal meaning of the body as gift; and TOB 23, an integral vision of man and woman in marriage.

Section 1 of part 4 then examines the mission of the different members of the family in building a communion of persons: the mother (22–23), the father (25), the children (26), and the elderly (27). In treating the mission of the mother, John Paul II insists that wives/mothers have the right and capacity to undertake all public functions, but their essential and indispensable role within the family must be honored and respected, and the uniquely important contributions they make to civilization as mothers and nurturers of life within the home must especially be recognized and honored (23.2). He emphasizes that wives and mothers must "*not in practice [be] compelled* to work outside the home," so that "their families can live and prosper in a dignified way even when they themselves devote their full time to their own family" (23.4).

In the brief treatment given to men/fathers, John Paul II emphasizes that the husband/father has a unique and indispensable role to play as the leader of the family. Although he does not call the husband/father the head of the family, he assigns him the role of *leader*. As the one called upon to reveal and relive "on earth the very Fatherhood of God," the husband/father has the responsibility to secure the unity of the family in carrying out the role entrusted to it (25.5). Moreover "efforts must be made to restore socially the conviction that the place and task of the father in and for the family is of unique and irreplaceable importance" (25.4).

Although these paragraphs of this section of part 2 do not explicitly echo themes from TOB, it is nonetheless true, it seems to me, that what is said about mother and father in TOB undergirds what is said here in *Familiaris Consortio*. Perhaps of more immediate relevance to these paragraphs are the catecheses devoted to conjugal spirituality, TOB 126–133.

2. Serving Life (28–41)

This theme of *Familiaris Consortio* is magnificently developed in TOB, especially in catecheses 118–125, where John Paul defends the teaching of *Humanae Vitae*; develops an argument to show that contraception is intrinsically evil because it violates the "language of the body," the "gift" of the spouses to one another; and likewise shows why recourse to the rhythm of fertility is, both anthropologically and morally, utterly different from recourse to contraception. Let us now look closely at the material found in numbers 28–41 of this great document.

"The fundamental task of the family is to serve life, to actualize in history the original blessing of the Creator — that of transmitting by procreation the divine image from person to person" (28.2). Precisely for this reason, openness to life is a necessary condition of true conjugal love and a sign of its authenticity (28.3, 29.3). This demands respect for the Church's teaching on the regulation of fertility. John Paul II, with Vatican II and Paul VI, insists that there can be no true contradiction between the divine law on transmitting life and that of fostering conjugal love (33.4). God's plan and conjugal love are at the root of the inseparable connection willed by

God and are not lawful for man on his own initiative to separate between the unitive and procreative meanings of the conjugal act (32.3). Indeed, John Paul II, in a most perceptive passage in this section, emphasizes that there is a radical "*difference, both anthropological and moral,* between contraception and recourse to the rhythm of the cycle," a difference ultimately rooted in "two irreconcilable concepts of the human person and of human sexuality" (32.6).

Many people seem to find it difficult to see any moral difference between contraception and "recourse to the rhythms of the cycle" as a means of avoiding a pregnancy when there is a good reason to do so, for instance, the mother's life or health. But there is a great difference. Their reasoning can be summarized as follows: *Major premise*: All contraception prevents conception. *Minor premise*: NFP (natural family planning, or "recourse to the rhythms of fertility") prevents conception. *Conclusion*: NFP ("recourse to the rhythms …") is contraception. That is like arguing: *Major premise*: All eagles are birds. *Minor premise*: Crows are birds. *Conclusion*: Crows are eagles. You can see that the reasoning is fallacious. The syllogism is invalid because neither premise makes a statement about the entire class of birds. So the subjects of the major and minor premise cannot be equated. In other words, knowing that both crows and eagles are birds doesn't tell us how crows and eagles are related. The same is true in regard to contraception and NFP. In both cases the *further* end for which the couple chooses either to contracept or practice NFP (what John Paul II here calls "recourse to the rhythms of fertility") is the same. But the *proximate* end chosen to reach this end is different. An example helps to clarify this. If a person needs money, there is a big difference, morally speaking, between working for a salary and stealing money. The goal is the same, but the means used to obtain it make all the difference. The same is true for contraception and NFP.

Contraception is rooted in a dualistic anthropology that sharply distinguishes between a human being as a "person," that is, as a conscious and autonomous subject, and a human being as a "body." That is why along with its "ends-justify-the-means" moral theory, contraception is at the root of the culture of death. In *Evangelium Vitae*, 19, Pope John Paul II identified the roots of the culture of death. He included among these roots a certain mentality. This mentality would recognize "as a subject of rights only the *person* who enjoys full or at least incipient autonomy and who emerges from a state of total dependence on others." He also criticized the "mentality which tends to *equate personal dignity with the capacity for verbal and explicit,* or at least perceptible, *communication.*" Thus, in this view, only those human beings who are "autonomous agents" with the "capacity for perceptible communication" are truly *persons.* This mentality looks on unborn babies, newly born babies, and mentally impaired individuals as living human bodies, but *not* as persons with rights. As we shall see in chapter 3, on the theology of the body, the overriding purpose of TOB is precisely a *defense of the reality of the human body as integral to the being of the human person,* in explicit opposition to the dualistic notion of the person, rooted in the Cartesian-Baconian dichotomy between the consciously experiencing person and his or her body, conceived as an instrument of the person. In this view, for example, an individual in the so-called vegetative state is biologically alive, but life has outlived its usefulness to the "person" who used to need it. That "person" is already dead or as good as dead, and surely is better off dead than alive — according to proponents of the culture of death.

3. Participating in the Development of Society (42–48)

"The family is by nature and vocation open to other families and to society, and undertakes its social role" (42.3). From that "the rights and duties" of the family vis-à-vis the larger society derive.

The basic point is that the family is the "foundation" of society and "nourishes it continually through its service to life … it is within the family that [citizens] find the first school of the social virtues that are the animating principle of the existence and development of society itself" (42.2). Thus the "first and fundamental contribution" of the family to society is "the very experience of communion and sharing that should characterize the family's daily life" (43.1). The Pope insists that the Christian family, to carry out its mission here, must engage in works of social service, especially by means of hospitality, both spiritual and material (44.2–4).

Although, as noted earlier, the catecheses in TOB do not seem *directly* to bear on what is written here, there is nonetheless a very strong *indirect* relationship. I believe that what John Paul says in TOB 94–102, reflecting on Paul's teaching in Ephesians on marriage, on marriage as the primordial sacrament that in Christ becomes a sacrament of redemption, and on the relationship of Christian spouses vis-à-vis the entire community, has great relevance to this part of *Familiaris Consortio*.

Just as the family is to serve society, so too society has a *grave obligation* to assist and support the family. John Paul II called for the issuance of a *charter of family rights*, and the Holy See published this on October 22, 1983.[1] *Familiaris Consortio* lists many of these (46), among them the right to found a family and to exercise responsibility in transmitting life; the right to demand protection of the intimacy of married life and the stability of the marriage bond; the right to educate children according to one's religious beliefs; and the right of a family to a family wage.

4. Sharing in the Life and Mission of the Church (49–64)

This section[2] is a short treatise on the Christian family as the "domestic church." John Paul II affirmed that the Christian family participates in the life and mission of the Church by sharing in the *prophetic, priestly, and kingly* mission of Christ, precisely because it is a: "1) believing and evangelizing community, 2) a community in dialogue with God, and 3) a community at the service of man" (50.5).

The Family as a Believing and Evangelizing Community: Its Prophetic Role

The Christian family shares in Christ's prophetic mission *"by welcoming and announcing the word of God"* (51.1). Thus the first requirement of Christian spouses and parents is faith, because "only in faith can they discover and admire with joyful gratitude the dignity to which God has deigned to raise marriage and the family, making them a sign and meeting place of the loving covenant between God and man, between Jesus Christ and his bride, the Church" (51.2).

The driving force of the Christian family is the love specific to spouses, but Christian spouses know through faith that their love is a sign and real participation in the love of God and in his redemptive power. God, who through faith "called the couple *to* marriage, continues to call them *in* marriage" (51.5). "In and through the events, problems, difficulties, and circumstances of everyday life, God comes to them, revealing and presenting the concrete 'demands' of their sharing in the love of Christ for his Church in the particular family, social, and ecclesial situation in which they find themselves" (51.5).

Faith thus heard and experienced in love makes the Christian family a fire that sheds its light on many other families (cf. 52). This prophetic mission of the family, John Paul II emphasizes, is the dynamic expression of its inner identity; the family carries this mission out by being faithful to its own proper being as a community of life and love: the "apostolic mission of the family is rooted in baptism and receives from the grace of the sacrament of marriage new strength to transmit the faith, to sanctify and transform our present society according to God's plan" (52.2).

The prophetic apostolate of the family has two characteristics. First, it is exercised within the family itself by encouraging and helping family members to live fully their Christian vocation. The Holy Father notes that "just as in the Church the work of evangelization can never be separated from the sufferings of the apostle, so in the Christian family parents must face with courage and great interior serenity the difficulties that their ministry of evangelization sometimes encounters in their own children" (53.3). Second, this prophetic and evangelizing apostolate, begun within the family itself, includes the "task of defending and spreading the faith, a task that has its roots in baptism and confirmation, and makes Christian married couples and parents witnesses of Christ 'to the ends of the earth,' missionaries, in the true and proper sense, of love and life" (54.2). One form of this missionary activity, John Paul II observes,

> can be exercised even within the family. This happens when some member of the family does not have the faith or does not practice it with consistency. In such a case the other

members must give him or her a living witness of their own
faith in order to encourage and support him or her along the
path towards full acceptance of Christ the Savior. (54.3)

The Family as a Community in Dialogue with God: Its Priestly Role

John Paul II begins his presentation of this essential task of
the Christian family by reminding us that marriage is a sacrament of mutual sanctification and of worship and that the love
of Christian spouses has been judged by the Lord, as Vatican
Council II had noted earlier, "worthy of special gifts, healing,
perfecting and exalting gifts of grace and of charity" (56.1).
Moreover, "the gift of Jesus Christ is not exhausted in the
actual celebration of the sacrament of marriage, but rather
accompanies the married couple throughout their lives" (56.2).

Precisely because Christian marriage is a sacrament of
mutual sanctification, the universal call of all Christians to
holiness is, for Christian spouses and parents, "specified by the
sacrament they have celebrated and is carried out concretely
in the realities proper to their conjugal and family life" (56.3).
John Paul II then emphasizes the *sacramental foundation* of
the sanctity demanded of spouses. Holiness is not easy, and it
lies beyond merely human powers. To sanctify themselves,
their children, and the world in which they live, Christian
spouses must have recourse to the sources of divine grace, in
particular the Eucharist and Reconciliation. Just as love is the
proper power of the family and participation in Christ's love
is what defines the Christian family, so the Eucharist is the
living fountain of Christian married and family life:

> The Eucharist is the very source of Christian marriage. The
> Eucharistic Sacrifice, in fact, represents Christ's covenant of
> love with the Church, sealed with his blood on the cross....

The Eucharist is a fountain of charity. In the Eucharistic gift of charity the Christian family finds the foundation and soul of its "communion" and its "mission." (57.2)

In addition, it is through the sacrament of Reconciliation that "the married couple and the other members of the family are led to an encounter with God, who is 'rich in mercy,' who bestows on them his love which is more powerful than sin, and who reconstructs and brings to perfection the marriage covenant and the family communion" (58.3).

By keeping close to Christ through the sacraments of the Eucharist and of Reconciliation and by prayer, the Christian family can discover family life itself, in all its circumstances,

as a call from God and lived as a filial response to his call. Joys and sorrows, hopes and disappointments, births and birthday celebrations, wedding anniversaries of the parents, departures, separations and homecomings, important and far-reaching decisions, the death of those who are dear, etc. — all of these mark God's loving intervention in the family's history. They should be seen as suitable moments for thanksgiving, for petition, for trusting abandonment of the family into the hands of their common Father in heaven. (59.3)

The Family as a Community at the Service of Humankind: Its Kingly Mission

The Christian family exercises this mission by putting itself at the service of others, as Christ did and as he asks his disciples to do (63.4). "The law of Christian life is to be found not in a written code, but in the personal action of the Holy Spirit who inspires and guides the Christian" (63.2). For Christian spouses and their families, the guide and rule of life is the Spirit of Jesus, the evangelical law of love. Thus, "inspired and sustained by the new commandment of love, the Christian family welcomes, respects, and serves every human being, considering each one in his or her dignity as a person and as a child of God" (64.1). This profound respect for the dignity of human persons must be shown first within the family itself — among husband and wife and their children,

> through a daily effort to promote a truly personal community, initiated and fostered by an inner communion of love. This way of life should then be extended to the wider circle of the ecclesial community of which the Christian family is a part ... [and ultimately this] love, too, goes beyond our brothers and sisters of the same faith since "everybody is my brother or sister." In each individual, especially in the poor, the weak, and those who suffer or are unjustly treated, love knows how to discover the face of Christ, and discover a fellow human being to be loved and served. (64.2–3)

John Paul II's Catecheses on the Theology of the Body: "Man and Woman He Created Them"[1]

The introduction to this chapter provides basic information about Pope John Paul II's catecheses on the theology of the body. I then consider:

1. The twofold purpose, structure, and argument of these catecheses;

2. The spousal meaning of the body in God's original plan (part 1, chapter 1 of TOB);

3. The spousal meaning of the body in our struggle with concupiscence (part 1, chapter 2 of TOB);

4. The fulfillment of marriage and the spousal meaning of the body in the resurrection (part 1, chapter 3 of TOB);

5. The function of the spousal meaning of the body in the sacrament (part 2, chapters 1, 2, and 3).

Introduction: Dates of Addresses in the "Theology of the Body" and Michael Waldstein's English Translation Based on the John Paul II Archives

From September 5, 1979, through November 28, 1984, John Paul II gave a series of Wednesday audiences on "The Theology of the Body." In 2006 Pauline Books & Media published a new translation of these addresses in a volume entitled *Man and Woman He Created Them: A Theology of the Body*. This new and much needed translation, expertly done by Michael Waldstein, is based on the archives of the John Paul II Foundation at Dom Polski in Rome. Waldstein uses the divisions and titles of the different parts of the theology of the body provided by John Paul II himself. Waldstein discovered these in a Polish manuscript that John Paul II had written before he was elected pope, and which he used as the basis for his papal audiences. These divisions and titles, encompassing the entire work, its structure, and argument are, Waldstein believes, superior to the view of its structure and argument provided by the division into "cycles" in the earlier versions of the text.

Many readers, however, may be more familiar with the older and widely used division of the text into six cycles. The chapters into which John Paul II divided the text correspond to the six cycles in the earlier English translation. Each of the 133 audiences found in the new translation is indicated by its number, followed by the paragraph number within that address. Thus 12.2 refers to the twelfth audience and to the second paragraph in that audience. John Paul II divided the text into two parts, each subdivided into three chapters:

1. The Twofold Purpose, Structure, and Argument of Theology of the Body

Purpose

TOB has a twofold purpose. The first is to defend the reality of the human body, a truth crucial to an adequate anthropology or understanding of the human person as a creature whose body is integral to his being as a person. This great truth is central to the Christian faith. It was repudiated in the early Christian centuries by the Gnostics and Manichaeans, and that repudiation was reinforced in Western culture by the dualistic anthropology of Bacon and Descartes. This dualistic anthropology regards the human body as mere matter, part of the subpersonal world over which the "subject/person" has dominion and as such is itself not personal (see Waldstein, pp. 94–95). In TOB John Paul II was at pains, as Waldstein points out, to show that the anthropology underlying the defense of contraception mounted by the authors of the celebrated "Majority Papers" of the Papal Commission on the regulation of birth (released to the press in 1967) is the same as the dualistic anthropology at the heart of the Cartesian divorce of the "person" from his/her body (pp. 100–103).

The second purpose of TOB is to defend the teaching of *Humanae Vitae*. John Paul II himself comments on this purpose especially in the last Wednesday audience (TOB 133). There, as Waldstein notes, John Paul "points to the encyclical *Humanae Vitae* as the true focus of TOB as a whole." Thus the Holy Father declared in that address:

> The catecheses devoted to *Humanae Vitae* constitute only one small part, the final part, of those that dealt with the redemption of the body and the sacramentality of marriage. If I draw particular attention precisely to these final catecheses, I do so not only because the topic discussed by them is more closely connected with our present age, but first of all because *it is from this topic that the questions spring* that run in some way through the whole of our reflections. It follows that this final part [concerning *Humanae Vitae*] is not artificially added to the whole, but is organically and homogeneously united with it. In some sense, that part, which in the overall disposition is located at the end, is at the same time found at the beginning of that whole. This is important from the point of view of structure and method. (TOB 133.4, p. 662; all emphasis in the text of TOB, unless noted, is in the original.) (cited by Waldstein, pp. 99–100)

These are the reasons why the purpose of TOB was to defend the teaching of *Humanae Vitae* in particular; in that encyclical Paul VI repudiated the Cartesian separation of the person/subject from his own body and appealed to an "integral vision" of the human person. To defend the encyclical and to provide the needed "integral vision," John Paul II in TOB offered a "rereading of the 'theology of the body' in the 'truth,'" i.e., in the light of Christ's incarnation and revelation of man to man himself. Waldstein closes this part of his introduction:

> To conclude, the purpose of the theology of the body is to defend the body against its alienation from the person in Cartesian rationalism. Put positively, the purpose is to show the divine plan for human spousal love, to show the goodness and beauty of the whole sexual sphere against its cheapening in the "objective, scientific" way of looking at nature. God's plan and its renewal by Christ, the redeemer, is imprinted deeply within the bodily nature of the person as a pre-given language of self-giving and fruitfulness. For the person to live sexuality in an authentic manner is to speak spousal love in conformity with this truth of the language of the body. True human fulfillment in the sexual sphere can be found only by following this divine plan for human love. This is why the defense of *Humanae Vitae* is so important, important for the good of the human person. "*The fundamental problem* the encyclical [*Humanae Vitae*] presents is the viewpoint of the *authentic development of the human person;* such development should be measured, as a matter of principle, by the measure of ethics and not only of technology." (TOB 133.3, p. 105)

Structure

The titles John Paul II gave to the whole (see above under "Introduction") show us how the first two parts ("The Words of Christ" and "The Sacrament") are interrelated and serve the overall purpose of TOB. This is evident from a significant passage from the final address, in which John Paul II declares, "The whole of the catecheses that I began more than four years ago and that I conclude today can be grasped under the title, 'Human Love in the Divine Plan,' or with greater precision, 'The Redemption of the Body and the Sacramentality of

Marriage'" (TOB 133.1, p. 659). Commenting on this passage, Waldstein says:

> The overall title mentions a single subject, "Human Love in the Divine Plan," while the subtitle has two parts, "The Redemption of the Body" and "The Sacramentality of Marriage." Since John Paul II says in the text quoted above that Part 2 is about "the sacramentality of marriage," one is led to assume that Part 1 is about "the redemption of the body." The Conclusion of Part 1 (TOB 86) confirms this assumption. It focuses on "the redemption of the body." At the very end of that Conclusion, John Paul II writes, "Everything we have tried to do in the course of our meditations in order to understand the words of Christ has its definitive foundation in the mystery of the redemption of the body." (TOB 86.8, p. 110)

Argument

In John Paul's TOB the redemption of the body is the end that determines all steps. In many ways part 1 ("The Words of Christ") itself offers a theology of the body. "Since the 'redemption of the body' is the final end considered by a theology of the body," Waldstein writes, "reflection on it implies a complete theology of the body in all its essential articulations" (pp. 110–111). He then cites an important passage from TOB in which John Paul II declares:

> To understand all that "the redemption of the body" implies according to Romans, an authentic theology of the body is necessary. We have attempted to build one, appealing first of all to the words of Christ. The constitutive elements of the theology of the body are contained in what Christ says when he appeals to the "beginning" concerning the question of the indissolubility of marriage (see Mt 19:8), in what he says

about concupiscence when he appeals to the human heart in the Sermon on the Mount (see Mt 5:28), and also in what he says when he appeals to the resurrection (see Mt 22:30). Each one of these statements contains in itself a rich content of an anthropological as well as ethical nature. Christ speaks to man — and speaks about man, who is a "body" and is created as male and female in the image and likeness of God; he speaks about man, whose heart is subjected to concupiscence; and, finally, about man, before whom the eschatological perspective of the resurrection of the body opens up. (TOB 86.4, p. 460; cited by Waldstein on p. 111)

"This text is helpful," Waldstein writes,

for understanding the function of Part 1. When it analyzes the three words of Jesus from the point of view of "the redemption of the body," Part 1 presents all "the constitutive elements of the theology of the body." ... Part 2 deepens and unfolds Part 1. The redemption of the body is closely connected with the "spousal meaning of the body." In fact, the definitive redemption of the body is nothing other than the final and glorious realization of the spousal meaning of the body in the resurrection and beatific vision (see TOB 67–68). From the very beginning, the spousal meaning of the body is "sacramental." It is a sign that manifests and communicates holiness (TOB 19.3–6). It signifies the covenant between God and his people, between Christ and the Church, and ultimately the mystery of mysteries, namely, the communion between the divine persons in the Trinity. For this reason, after a first comprehensive account of the redemption of the body in Part 1, John Paul II deepens and unfolds this account in Part 2 by focusing on the "*sacramentum magnum*," the great mystery of love revealed in Ephesians 5. (pp. 111–112)

Thus, Waldstein concludes:

The main argument of TOB is thus very simple and clear. Its first step consists in unfolding the teaching of Jesus about the spousal meaning of the body (in its three dimensions: in God's original plan "from the beginning"; in the present struggle with concupiscence; and in the future fulfillment by the resurrection). Its second step consists in observing how this spousal meaning functions in the great sacrament of love, particularly in the language of the body that is the effective sign of this sacrament. Its third step consists in showing that *Humanae Vitae* simply asks men and women to reread this language of the body in the truth. The persuasive power of the argument lies in its ability to bring the teaching of Jesus to bear on the question of the genuine development and happiness of the human person. Jesus' teaching has an *inner* persuasive power, which lies in the beauty of God's plan for human love. (p. 124)

Now I will take up the three steps Waldstein mentions, beginning with the spousal meaning of the body.

2. The Spousal Meaning of the Body in God's Original Plan (TOB 1–23; Part 1, Chapter 1)

Christ's Response to the Pharisees

John Paul II begins his catechesis on TOB by taking as his starting point Christ's reply to the question raised by the Pharisees, "Is it lawful for a man to divorce his wife for any reason?", namely, "Have you not read that from the beginning *the Creator created them male and female* and said, *'For this reason a man will leave his father and his mother and unite with his wife, and the two will be one flesh?'* So it is that they are no longer two but one flesh. Therefore, what God has joined let man not separate" (Mt 19:3–6). Since Christ quoted Genesis in his reply, John Paul II says we must return to the "beginning" to discover God's loving plan for human persons, male and female. Christ makes it clear that Genesis 2.24 "states the principle of the unity and indissolubility of marriage as the very content of the word of God expressed in the most ancient revelation" (TOB 1.3, p. 132).

Original Solitude

Pope John Paul begins by analyzing the two creation accounts in Genesis. In doing so he introduces the concept of "original solitude" — a solitude common to both the male person and the female person — whereby man realizes he differs bodily from all other material beings insofar as he "names" the other animals and has dominion over them (see Gen 2:20), showing that he is "alone" as a person before God. In addition to this solitude there is the "solitude" the man person experiences because he is "alone" with no created person to share life with him as a suitable "partner" (see Gen 2:20) and then God makes for him a "woman" by framing her from the sleeping man's rib, "flesh of his flesh and bone of his bones," a person like himself (see Gen 2:21–23). Both these solitudes man comes to know through the reality of his own body, and the second discloses to him what John Paul II calls the "spousal meaning" of the body — i.e., the truth that the man person's body is meant to be a "gift" to the female person and her body is meant to be a gift to him. In his analyses of the creation accounts in Genesis 1 (attributed to the Elohist source) and Genesis 2 (attributed to the Yahwist source), John Paul II emphasizes that the human body reveals the human person and has a spousal meaning. The Holy Father introduces the first truth — that the human body reveals the human person — in commenting on

Genesis 2:18, which speaks of the man being alone. Here the issue is with the solitude of "'man' (male and female) and not only with the solitude of the man-male, caused by the absence of the woman.... [T]his *solitude has two meanings: one deriving from man's very nature,* that is, from his humanity ... and *the other deriving from the relationship between male and female*" (5.2, p. 147). The solitude deriving from man's very nature enables us:

> to *link man's original solitude with the awareness of the body,* through which man distinguishes himself from all the *animalia* and "separates himself" from them, and *through which* he is a *person.* One can affirm with certainty that man thus formed has at the same time the awareness and consciousness of the meaning of his own body. Moreover, [he has] this based on the experience of original solitude. (6.3, p. 152)

In short, man's awareness of his body as different from the bodies of other animals enables him to grasp the truth that he, alone among visible creatures, is a person, gifted with self-consciousness and self-determination.

The Holy Father perhaps most dramatically shows that the human body reveals the human person and in doing so also reveals the spousal meaning of the body when he considers the second meaning of man's "solitude" and reflects on the text of Genesis 2:18–24, which describes in poetic terms the "creation" of woman. "When the first man exclaims at the sight of the woman, 'she is flesh from my flesh and bone from my bones' (Gen 2:23), he simply affirms," the Pope says, "the human identity of both. By exclaiming this, he seems to say: *Look, a body that expresses the 'person'*" (14.4, p. 183).

Since the body expresses the person, and since persons are to be loved, an ethical consequence is that we must never express with our bodies anything unworthy of the person. The body is a beautiful manifestation of a human person in all his or her God-given dignity.

Original Nakedness and Original Unity

By "original nakedness" and "original unity," John Paul refers to the fact that, as Genesis 2:25 informs us, Adam (now the personal name of the first male person) and Eve (his wife) after her creation from his rib and before their "fall" (see Gen 3), were "naked, yet they felt no shame." John Paul also shows that the mystery of original human nakedness reveals the "spousal meaning of the body." In short, the male person's body is a sign of the gift of the male person to the female person and vice versa. Because of the spousal meaning of the body man, male and female, realizes that he can fulfill himself as a person only by giving himself to another in love, in the sincere gift of self. He realizes that his vocation is to love.

Reflecting once again on the first man's cry of joy, "she is flesh from my flesh and bone from my bones" (Gen 2:23), the Pope declares: "these words in some way express the subjectively beatifying beginning of man's existence in the world" (14.3, p. 182). "This beatifying 'beginning' of man's being and existing as male and female," John Paul II continues,

> is connected with the revelation and the discovery of the meaning of the body that is rightly called "spousal." ...We have already observed that after the words expressing the first joy of man's coming into existence as "male and female" (Gen 2:23) there follows the verse that establishes their conjugal unity (Gen 2:24), and then the one that attests the nakedness of both without reciprocal shame (Gen 2:25). That these verses face each other in such a significant way allows us to

speak *of revelation together with the discovery of the "spousal" meaning of the body in the mystery of creation.* (14.5, pp. 183–184)

The Sincere Gift of Self

In his introduction (p. 124), Waldstein calls the "gift of self" the "guiding star" for reading John Paul II's TOB. Citing the author Pascal Ide, Waldstein writes: "Gift expresses the essential truth of the human body."

In a beautiful passage, John Paul II says:

While in the mystery of creation the woman is the one who is "given" to the man, he on his part, in receiving her as a gift in the full truth of her person and femininity, enriches her by this very reception, and, at the same time, he too is enriched in this reciprocal relationship. The man is enriched not only through her, who gives her own person and femininity to him, but also by the gift of self. The man's act of self-dona-tion, in answer to that of the woman, is for him himself an enrichment; in fact, it is here that *the specific essence,* as it were, of *his masculinity is manifested, which, through the reality of the body and of its sex, reaches the innermost depth of "self-possession,"* thanks to which he is able both to give himself and to receive the gift of the other. The man, therefore, not only accepts the gift, but at the same time is welcomed as a gift by the woman in the self-revelation of the inner spiritual essence of his mas-culinity together with the whole truth of his body and his sex. When he is accepted in this way, he is enriched by this acceptance and welcoming of the gift of his own masculinity. It follows that such an acceptance, in which the man finds himself through the "sincere gift of self," becomes in him a source of a new and more profound enrichment of the woman with himself. The exchange is reciprocal and the mutual effects of the "sincere gift" and of "finding oneself" reveal themselves and grow in that exchange. (17.6, p. 197)

As this text shows, husbands and wives are meant to give and receive one another precisely in and through the spousal meaning of their bodies. This meaning reflects their sexual complementarity. It seems to me that John Paul's way of articulating the giving and receiving ("acceptance" is the term used in the text) has been well expressed by Robert Joyce, who says that both the man and the woman are to give and to receive in a loving way, but that the man is so constituted in his masculinity that he is emphatically inclined to "give in a receiving sort of way" whereas the woman is so constituted in her femininity that she is emphatically inclined to "receive in a giving sort of way." [2]

Spousal Meaning in God's Original Plan and Immunity from Shame

In a further memorable passage linking the original spousal meaning of the body to the absence of shame in the state of original innocence prior to the Fall (see Gen 2:25), John Paul says:

> Happiness is being rooted in Love. Original happiness speaks to us about the "beginning" of man, who emerged from love and initiated love. And this happened irrevocably, despite the subsequent sin and death. In his time, Christ was to be a witness to this irreversible love of the Creator and Father, which had already expressed itself in the mystery of creation and in the grace of original innocence. For this reason, also the common "beginning" of man and woman, that is, the original truth of their body in masculinity and femininity, to which Genesis 2:25 turns our attention, does not know shame. One can define this "beginning" also as the original and beatifying immunity from shame as the result of love. (16.2, pp. 190–191)

This immunity from shame directs us to the mystery of man's original innocence, of his existence prior to the knowledge of good and evil and almost "outside" it. The fact that man exists in this way before breaking the first covenant with his Creator belongs to the fullness of the mystery of creation. Why is this so? John Paul II explains:

> If creation is a gift given to man ... then *its fullness* and deepest dimension is *determined by grace*, that is, by participation in the inner life of God himself, in his holiness. In man, this holiness is also the inner foundation and source of his original innocence. With this concept — and more precisely with that of "original justice" — theology defines the state of man before original sin. (16.3, p. 191)

We have already seen that in the state of original justice, before the Fall, the man and the woman were naked yet had no shame because the spousal meaning of their bodies was perfectly revealed to them.

Of crucial importance is that it is "this consciousness of the body — or, even better, *consciousness of the meaning of the body ... [that] reveals the distinctive character of original innocence*" (16.3, p. 191). In fact:

> The body itself of each is a witness of this characteristic, in some way an "eyewitness." It is significant that the statement contained in Genesis 2:25 — about reciprocal nakedness free from shame — is a statement unique in its kind in the whole Bible, so much so that it was never to be repeated. On the contrary, we can quote many texts in which nakedness is linked with shame or even, in a still stronger sense, with "defilement." (16.3, pp. 191–192; in footnote 1, John Paul II refers to Hos 1:2 and Ezek 23:26, 29 as texts to illustrate this)

Original innocence "is that which 'radically, that is, *at its very root' excludes the shame of the body* in the relationship between man and woman, that which *eliminates the necessity of this shame in man*, in his *heart* or his *conscience*" and it refers above all to "the interior state of the human 'heart,' of the human will" (16.4, p. 193).

However, as a result of the fall, as we have seen already, the "spousal meaning of the body" is, as it were, "veiled." As a result, concupiscence entered the human heart and the body is in need of redemption.

The Perspective of Redemption

But, and this is most important, in his fourth audience John Paul II insists that the "beginning" to which Christ referred indicates not only man's creation but must be seen within the perspective of the "redemption of the body." In a remarkable text, he writes:

> [A]lready in the context of the same Yahwist text of Genesis 2 and 3, we witness the moment in which man, male and female, after having broken the original covenant with his Creator, receives the first promise of redemption in the words of the so-called Protoevangelium ... and begins to live *in the theological perspective of redemption* ... historical man ... participates not only *in the history of human sinfulness* ... but he also participates *in the history of salvation*.... He is ... open to the mystery of this redemption realized in Christ and through Christ. Paul ... expresses this perspective of redemption, in which "historical man" lives, when he writes: "We ourselves, who have the first fruits of the Spirit, groan inwardly while we wait for ... the redemption of our bodies" (Rom 8:23).... If that "beginning" indicated only the creation of man as "male and female," if ... Christ only led his interlocutors across the boundary of man's state of sin to original innocence and did not open at the same time the perspective of a "redemption of the body," his answer would not at all be

understood adequately. Precisely *this perspective of the redemption of the body guarantees the continuity and the unity* between man's hereditary state of sin and his original innocence, although within history this innocence has been irremediably lost by him. (4.3, pp. 143–144)

The Sacramental Principle

John Paul, in speaking of the "spousal meaning" of the body brings out what we can call *the sacramental principle and sacramentality of the body*. By the "sacramental principle" is meant the truth that all visible reality is, in a sense, a "sacrament" insofar as it points to, i.e. is a "sign" of, the invisible God, the creator. By "sacramentality of the body" is meant the truth that the human body not only points to or is a sign of the personhood of man, male and female, but makes this reality present here and now in the world. He emphasizes that

man enters into the world and into the innermost guiding thread of his future and his history with the consciousness of the spousal meaning of his own body, of his own masculinity and femininity. Original innocence says that this meaning is conditioned "ethically" and … that … it constitutes the future of human ethos. (18.4, p. 200)

He likewise points out that "Genesis 2:24 notes that the two, man and woman, were created for marriage" (18.5, p. 200). Speaking of man's situation after the Fall, after original sin, he says that after sin "the discovery of the spousal meaning of the body was to cease being for them a simple reality of revelation and grace," but nonetheless, "this meaning was to *remain as a task given to man by the ethos of the gift*, inscribed in the depth of the human heart" (19.2, p. 202). In fact, "From that spousal meaning, human love was to be formed in its interior truth and authentic subjectivity. And even through the veil of shame, man was to continuously discover himself in it as the guardian of the mystery of the subject, that is, of the freedom of the gift, in order to defend this freedom from any reduction to the position of a mere object" (ibid.). To illustrate this, a married man or woman is ready to postpone gratifying even legitimate desires if seeking gratification here and now would require regarding the other not as a person to be loved but as a body (object) to be consumed or used.

In this nineteenth address, too, the Pope says that since man appears in the visible world as the "highest expression of the divine gift," bearing within himself "the inner dimension of the gift," it follows that in the dimension of the gift:

> A *primordial* sacrament is constituted, understood as a *sign that* efficaciously *transmits in the visible world the invisible mystery hidden in God from eternity*. And this is the mystery of Truth and Love, the mystery of divine life, in which man really participates.... The sacrament, as a visible sign, is constituted with man, inasmuch as he is a "body," through his "visible" masculinity and femininity. The body, in fact, and only the body, is capable of making visible what is invisible: the spiritual and the divine. It has been created to transfer into the visible reality of the world the mystery hidden from eternity in God, and thus to be a sign of it. (19.4, p. 203)

From this it should be evident that for John Paul II the human body is itself the "primordial sacrament." In fact, he goes on to say in 19.5, page 203:

> In man, created in the image of God, the very sacramentality of creation, the sacramentality of the world was thus in some way revealed. In fact, through his bodiliness, his masculinity and femininity, man becomes a visible sign of the economy of Truth and Love, which has its source in God himself, and was revealed already in the mystery of creation.

Moreover, man fully is the image of God in the communion of persons — male and female — that we call marriage, so that marriage itself must also be regarded as the "primordial" sacrament (see TOB 19.5). These truths are a powerful expression of the *sacramental principle* of Catholic faith, and it shows the importance of the *theology of the body* insofar as the human body itself is a "sacrament" of the divine gift.

Knowledge and Procreation

In audiences 20, 21, and 23 the Pope is concerned with analyzing the biblical meaning of "knowledge" and procreation, the mystery of woman as revealed in motherhood, and the cycle of knowledge and generation and the perspective of death in order to show their bearing on the theology of the body.

"Adam knew Eve his wife, and she conceived and bore Cain, saying, 'I have gotten a man with the help of the Lord.' And again, she bore his brother Abel" (Gen 4:1–2). In his commentary on this passage, John Paul maintains that a new depth of meaning and the "deepest essence of the reality of married life" emerge, a meaning and an essence deriving "from all the meanings" he has hitherto analyzed in Genesis, i.e., the body as revelatory of the person, the spousal meaning of the body, and the reality of the "gift" in the original state of innocence when "they were naked and were not ashamed." Let us remember that "Adam knew Eve" *after* the Fall. But see precisely how the Pope comments on this text:

> If we connect that first fact of the birth of a man on earth with knowledge, we do so on the basis of the literal translation of the text, according to which conjugal "union" is defined precisely as "knowledge": in fact the translation just quoted says, "*Adam united himself* with Eve his wife," while

according to the letter one should translate "*knew his wife*," which seems to correspond more exactly to the Semitic term *yada*. One can see in this a sign of the poverty of the ancient language, which lacked varied expressions for defining differentiated facts. Nevertheless, it remains significant that *the situation in which husband and wife unite* so intimately among themselves *as to form "one flesh" was defined as "knowledge."* In this way, in fact, from the very poverty of the language there seems to emerge a specific depth of meaning that derives from all the meanings analyzed up to this point. (20.2, p. 206)

... With that biblical "knew" ... we find ourselves face to face with, on the one hand, the direct expression of human intentionality (because it is proper to knowledge) and, on the other hand, the whole reality of conjugal life and conjugal union, in which man and woman become "one flesh." When it speaks of "knowledge" here ... the Bible indicates the deepest essence of the reality of shared married life. This essence appears as a component and, at the same time, as a result of the meanings the traces of which we have been trying to follow from the beginning of our study; it is, in fact, part of the consciousness of the meaning of one's own body.... In Genesis 4:1, when they become one flesh, the man and the woman experience the meaning of their bodies in a particular way. Together, they thus become one single subject, as it were, of that act and that experience, although they remain two really distinct subjects in this unity. This authorizes us in some sense to affirm that "the husband knows his wife" or that both "know each other" reciprocally. Thus, they reveal themselves to one another with *that specific depth of their own human* "I," which *precisely reveals itself also through their sex*, their masculinity and femininity. And thus, in a singular way, the woman "is given" in the mode of knowledge to the man, and he to her. (20.4, p. 207)

"Knowledge" and Procreation's Relevance to the Theological Significance of the Human Body

In addition, the "knowledge" proper to the conjugal act is intimately linked to procreation. "Procreation brings it about that 'the man and the woman (his wife)' *know each other reciprocally in the 'third,' originated by both*" (21.4, p. 211). The "knowledge" spoken of reveals to the man and the woman

> the new man, in whom both, the man and the woman, again recognize each other, their humanity, their living image.... "Knowledge" in the biblical sense signifies that man's "biological" determination, on the part of his body and his sex, is no longer something passive but reaches a level and content specific to self-conscious and self-determining persons; therefore, it brings with it a particular consciousness of the meaning of the human body bound to fatherhood and motherhood. (21.4, pp. 211–212)

While recognizing the "deep differences between the state of original innocence and the state of man's hereditary sinfulness," John Paul II nonetheless brings this audience to a close with the following significant comment that in many ways summarizes the relevance of procreation to understanding the theological significance of the human body:

> The "knowledge" about which Genesis 4.1 speaks is *the act that* originates being, or, *in union with the Creator, establishes a new human being in existence.* In his transcendental solitude, the first man took possession of the visible world, created for him, by knowing and giving their names to living beings (*animalia*). Since the same man, as male and female, knows himself reciprocally in this specific community-communion of persons, in which man and woman unite so closely with each other that they become "one flesh," he constitutes humanity, that is, he confirms and renews the existence of man as image

of God. Every time, both man and woman take this image again, so to speak, from the mystery of creation and transmit it "with the help of God-Yahweh." The words of Genesis that bear witness to the first birth of man on earth contain, at the same time, everything that one can and should say about the dignity of human procreation. (21.7, pp. 213–214)

John Paul II maintains that the revelation of the body found in Genesis, particularly in chapter 3, which deals with man's fall and the change from the state of innocence to that of sinfulness, "shows with impressive obviousness that the cycle of 'knowledge-generation,' rooted so deeply in the power of the human body, has been subjected, after sin, to the law of suffering and death." This cycle after sin was so subjected because of the suffering a woman experiences in giving birth and in the fact that she, her husband, and their children are all subject to death, the penalty for original sin.

The Holy Father then continues:

The horizon of death opens before man together with the *revelation of the generative meaning of the body* in the spouses' act of reciprocal "knowledge." And so, the first man, the male, gives to his wife the name Eve, "because she was the mother of all the living" (Gen 3:20), when he had already heard the words of the sentence that determined the whole perspective of human existence "from within" the knowledge of good and evil. This perspective is confirmed by the words, "You will return to the earth, for out of it you were taken; dust you are, and to dust you shall return" (Gen 3:19). The radical character of this sentence is confirmed by the evidence of the experience of man's whole earthly history. The horizon of death extends over the whole perspective of human life on earth, a life that has been inserted into that original biblical cycle of "knowledge-generation." Man, who has broken the covenant with his Creator, gathering the fruit from the tree of the knowledge of good and evil, is cut off by God-Yahweh from the tree of life: "Now, let him not reach out his hand any more and take also from the tree of life, and eat, and live forever" (Gen 3:21). In this way, *the life given to man in the mystery of creation is not taken away*, but restricted by the limit of conceptions, of births, and of death, and further worsened by the perspective of hereditary sinfulness; yet *it is in some way given to him anew as a task in the same ever-recurring cycle.* (22.5, pp. 216–217; emphasis added)

In short, through "knowledge-generation" "historical" man realizes that despite his sinfulness and the death that it incurs, his own existence is a gift from God and that it is his mission, his honor, his privilege, to give it to new human persons. And it is a *bodily gift.*

Marriage in the Integral Vision of Man

John Paul II uses the twenty-third and final audience of the first chapter of TOB to summarize, in his own way, the integral vision of man necessary if we are to construct a theological anthropology, especially a "theology of the body," at the root of the Christian understanding of marriage and the family. This is the vision set forth in the "beginning" to which Christ referred his interlocutors asking about the issue of divorce. John Paul II sees in this "beginning" "the first inheritance of every human being in the world, man and woman, the first witness of human identity according to the revealed word, the first source of the certainty of his vocation as a person created in the image of God himself" (23.1, p. 219). John Paul II holds, moreover, that were the challenges to marriage raised by our contemporaries quite different from those posed by his interlocutors in the Gospels, Christ would again refer to the "beginning." In fact, he says, Christ "perhaps would do so all the more decidedly and essentially, inasmuch as man's inner and simultaneously cultural situation seems to move away from that beginning and assume forms and dimensions that diverge from the biblical image of the 'beginning' to points that are evidently ever more distant" (23.2, p. 219). Here he is, in effect, saying that what is needed today is a "re-evangelization," a proclamation that helps men and women, blinded by the culture of death that has come about as a result of a denigration of the reality of the human body, to realize that they are in fact living *bodies* of a unique kind.

An analysis of the "beginning" brings to our mind "fundamental and elementary truths about the human being as man and woman." The answer to the question about divorce given to us by an analysis of the beatifying beginning of human existence is, the Pope maintains, the answer through which

we gain insight into the very structure of human identity in the dimensions of the mystery of creation and, at the same time, in the perspective of the mystery of redemption. *Without this answer, one cannot build a theological anthropology and, in its context, a "theology of the body" from which also the fully Christian vision of marriage and the family originates.* (23.3, p. 220; emphasis added)

Continuing, the Pope says:

[T]he truth that is important for the integral vision of man reveals itself in a simpler and fuller way. This truth *concerns the meaning of the human body in the structure of the personal subject* [= the human person]. The reflection about these ancient texts allows us as a next step to extend this meaning to the whole sphere of human *intersubjectivity* [i.e., the truth that human persons must regard each other not as "objects" for use but as "persons" to be loved], especially in the perennial relationship between man and woman. In this reflection we gain a vantage point that we must necessarily place at the basis of the whole contemporary science about human sexuality in the biophysiological sense. [This science is valuable in itself, but if it is truly to help us, we must keep in mind what is fundamental and essentially personal in every man and woman and in their mutual relations. And it is here] that reflection on the ancient text of Genesis proves to be irreplaceable. It constitutes really the "beginning" of the theology of the body. The fact that *theology also includes the body should not* astonish or surprise anyone who is conscious of the mystery and reality of the Incarnation. Through the fact that the Word of God became flesh, the body entered theology ... through the main door. The Incarnation — and the redemption that flows from it — has also become the definitive source of the sacramentality of marriage. (23.4, p. 221; bracketed words are a paraphrase)

All who seek to find their vocation in marriage "are called first of all to make of this 'theology of the body,' whose 'beginning' we find in the first chapters of Genesis, the content of their lives and behavior" (23.5, p. 222). "How necessary is an accurate consciousness of the spousal meaning of the body, of its generative meaning, given that all that forms the content of the life of the spouses must always find its full and personal dimension in shared life, in behavior, in feelings!" (23.5, p. 222). John Paul also reminds us that the path along which Christ leads man, male and female, "in the sacrament of marriage, namely, the way of the 'redemption of the body,' must consist in *retrieving this dignity* [the dignity of the purity of heart open to the "gift" of the other] in which the true meaning of the human body, its meaning as personal and 'of communion' is fulfilled" (23.5, p. 222).

3. The Spousal Meaning of the Body in Our Struggle with Concupiscence (TOB 24–63; Part 1, Chapter 2)

The Sermon on the Mount and Concupiscence

John Paul II begins the second chapter of the first part of TOB by saying that he wishes to develop Christ's statement in the Sermon on the Mount, "You have heard that it was said, 'You shall not commit adultery.' But I say to you: Whoever looks at a woman to desire her [in a reductive way] has already committed adultery with her *in his heart*" (Mt 5:27–28). "This passage," he says, "has a key significance for the theology of the body" (24.1, p. 225). Christ's declaration here

> brings about *a fundamental revision of the way of understanding and carrying out the moral law of the Old Covenant....* Especially significant are the words ... by which Jesus declares, "Do not think that I have come to abolish the Law or the Prophets; I have not come to abolish but to fulfill." (Mt 5:17).... *The fulfillment of the law is the* underlying *condition* for this reign [the Kingdom of God] in the temporal dimension of human existence. It is a question, however, of a fulfillment that fully corresponds to the meaning of the law, of the Decalogue, of the single commandments. Only such a fulfillment *builds the justice that God, the Legislator, has willed.*" (24.1, pp. 226–227)

John Paul affirms that Christ's statement (Mt 5:27–28) along with his appeal to the "beginning" in Matthew 19:3–9 and Mark 10 must be considered "the key to the theology of the body" and that, like Matthew 19:3–9, it "has an explicitly normative character," confirming the Sixth Commandment and also determining "a fitting and full understanding" of this principle, which must now be "considered precisely in the light of the words of Matthew 5:17–20" (24.2, p. 227). Christ's appeal to the "beginning" is the key to TOB because it is in going to that beginning that we discover, as we have seen, that the human body reveals the human person and the truth that man fully images the Triune God only in the communion of persons, male and female, that is marriage. He then declares:

> we thus find ourselves at the heart of ethos, or, as it could be defined, the inner form, the soul, as it were, of human morality.... The morality in which the very meaning of being human is realized — which is, at the same time, the fulfillment of the law by the "superabounding" of justice through subjective vitality — is formed in the interior perception of values, from which duty is born as an expression of conscience, as an answer of one's own personal "I." (24.3, pp. 227–228)

In short, the Pope sees *the Sermon on the Mount, with Christ's fulfilling and deepening of the old law, as the heart or core of "Christian" morality.* He also points out that in addition to the Sixth Commandment the Decalogue has the Ninth: "You shall not desire your neighbor's wife," and that in the Sermon on the Mount Christ connects the Sixth and Ninth Commandments: "You have heard that it was said, 'You shall not commit adultery.' But I say to you: Whoever looks at a woman to desire her has already committed adultery with her in his heart." Here Jesus points out "the dimension of interior action" that "finds its visible expression in the 'act of the body,' the act in which man and woman share, contrary to the law of the exclusivity of marriage" (24.4, p. 228).

Old Testament casuistry found "loopholes" in the Sixth Commandment and the kind of compromises prompting

Moses to allow divorce because of "hardness of heart," resulting in a distortion of God's intent in giving the commandment. Christ, by speaking of the concupiscent "look," shifts the essence of the problem by appealing to "the interior man" whom he seeks to form and whom he summons to rediscover the meaning of his existence as a bodily person.

The man to whom Christ appeals is "'historical' man, the one whose 'beginning' and 'theological prehistory'" were traced in the first twenty-three audiences. "This man is in some way 'each' man, 'every one' of us" (25.1). Christ addresses the "interior" man, and his words have "an explicit *anthropological content*: they touch those perennial meanings that constitute an 'adequate' anthropology" (25.2, p. 231). By "adequate anthropology" the Holy Father means an understanding of man and woman that recognizes that the human body is integral to the *being* of the human person. It is not understood as a conscious subject aware of itself as a self whose "body" is not integral to its being. This is the case for contemporary writers who separate the "person" from the body, for example, those who hold that not all living bodies, e.g., unborn children, are persons although they are indeed living human bodies. Because of their ethical content, Christ's words "constitute such an [adequate] anthropology and demand, so to speak, that man enters into his full image. Man — who is 'flesh,' and who, as male, remains through his body and his sex in relation with woman ... must, in the light of these words of Christ, find himself in his interior, in his 'heart'" (25.2, p. 231). But to rediscover and recover the spousal meaning of the body, the human person must know what is wrong with himself, namely lust or concupiscence. "Christ wants us ... to enter into the ... full ethical and anthropological [meaning of the statement about looking lustfully].... If we follow its footsteps, we can reach an understanding of the general truth about 'historical' man, valid also for the theology of the body" (25.5, p. 233).

Concupiscence and Shame

A key idea in TOB is that concupiscence "obscures" the spousal meaning of the body, and John Paul II develops this idea both in his reflections on the third chapter of Genesis, which tells us of the sin of the first man and its dreadful consequences for human existence, and on the teaching in the New Testament by Jesus in the Sermon on the Mount and in the Pauline literature on "concupiscence." In reflecting on the Genesis text, John Paul likewise highlights the contrast between the lack of shame over their nakedness experienced by Adam and Eve in the state of original innocence and on the shame over their nakedness they experience after their fall from grace.

Commenting on Genesis 3, the Pope writes:

> The man who picks the fruit of the tree of the knowledge of good and evil makes ... a fundamental choice and carries it through against the will of the Creator, God-Yahweh ... man turns his back on God-Love, on the "Father." ... He detaches his heart and cuts it off, as it were, from that which "comes from the Father": in this way, what is left in him "comes from the world." (26.4, pp. 236–237)

> "Then the eyes of both were opened, and they realized that they were naked" (Gen 3:6).... Genesis 3:6 speaks explicitly about the birth of shame in connection with sin. That shame is, as it were, the first source of the manifestation in man — in both the man and the woman — of what "does not come from the Father, but from the world." (26.5, pp. 237–238)

Because of their shame man and woman find it necessary to hide from God. "The need to hide shows that, in the depth of the shame they feel before each other as the immediate fruit of the tree of the knowledge of good and evil, a sense of fear before God has matured: a fear previously unknown" (27.1, p. 238).

> A certain fear is always part of the very essence of shame; nevertheless, original shame reveals its character in a particular way: "I was afraid, because I am naked." We realize that something deeper is at stake here than mere bodily shame.... With his shame about his own nakedness, the man seeks to cover the true origin of fear by indicating the effect so as not to name the cause.... In reality, what shows itself through "nakedness" is man deprived of participation in the Gift, man alienated from the Love that was the source of the original gift, the source of the fullness of good intended for the creature. This man, according to the formulas of the Church's theological teaching, was deprived of the supernatural and preternatural gifts that were part of his "endowment" before sin; in addition, *he suffered damage in what belongs to nature itself, to humanity in the original fullness "of the image of God."* (27.1–2, pp. 239–240; emphasis added)

Shame is the sign that a radical change has come over man. In the state of original innocence nakedness did not express a lack but rather a full acceptance of the body in all its human and personal truth. It was "a faithful witness and a perceptible verification of man's original 'solitude' in the world, while becoming at the same time, through masculinity and femininity, a transparent component of reciprocal giving in the communion of persons" (27.3, p. 241). But now, as a result of original sin and of the concupiscence that has entered his "heart," man has lost, in a way, "*the original certainty of the 'image of God,'* expressed in his body" (27.4, p. 241). This, John Paul II says, can be called the "cosmic shame" that man experienced with regard to his Creator.

In the biblical text this cosmic shame "gives up its place to another form of shame ... the shame produced in humanity itself," indeed a shame "*whose cause is found in humanity itself,*" an "immanent and relative shame":

> This is the shame of the woman "with regard to" man, and also of man "with regard to" woman: a reciprocal shame.... The Yahwist text seems to indicate explicitly the "sexual" character of this shame. "They sewed fig leaves together and made themselves loincloths." Nevertheless, we can ask ourselves whether the "sexual" aspect has only a "relative" character; in other words, whether it is a question of shame of one's own sexuality only in reference to the person of the other sex. (28.1, p. 243)

The Pope then clarifies the "immanent" and "relative" meanings of sexual shame: "Immanent shame" is the sexual shame the human person, male and female, manifests within the person, whereas "relative shame" is the shame the person experiences with regard to another person (see 28.1, p. 243). For instance, a husband experiences immanent shame when he is viewed by another as an object to be used and not a person to be loved, and he experiences relative shame when he regards his wife as an object and not a person.

The Holy Father maintains that although the text of Genesis 3:7 ("the eyes of both of them were opened...") seems to support the relative character of original shame, nonetheless deeper reflection

> allows us to discover its more immanent background. That shame, which shows itself without any doubt in the "sexual"

order, reveals *a specific difficulty in sensing the human essentiality of one's own body*, a difficulty man had not experienced in the state of original innocence. In this way, in fact, one can understand the words, "I was afraid, because I am naked." ...These words reveal a certain constitutive fracture in the human person's interior, *a breakup, as it were, of man's original spiritual and somatic unity*. (28.2, pp. 243–244)

This is a remarkable passage. Immanent shame makes it difficult for a person, man or woman, to realize that his/her body has a spousal meaning and as such is integral to his/her *being* as a person. In this passage, it seems to me, John Paul indicates the origin of a false dualistic anthropology that divorces the "person," or "conscious subject," from his own body, a dualism he later identifies, in *Evangelium Vitae*, as one of the roots of the "culture of death." As a matter of fact, the Pope continues, immanent shame:

contains such cognitive sharpness that it creates a fundamental disquiet in the whole of human existence: [T]he body is not subject to the spirit as in the state of original innocence, but carries within itself a constant hotbed of resistance against the spirit and threatens in some way man's unity as a person, that is, the unity of the moral nature that plunges its roots firmly into the very constitution of the person. The concupiscence of the body is a specific threat to the structure of self-possession and self-dominion, through which the human person forms himself. And it also constitutes a specific challenge for the person. In any case, *the man of concupiscence does not rule his own body in the same way, with the same simplicity and "naturalness" as the man of original innocence.* The structure of self-possession, which is essential for the person, is in some way shaken in him to its very foundations; he identifies himself anew with this structure in the degree to which he is continually ready to win it. (28.3, p. 244)

We could say that a man of concupiscence is possessed by his desires and does not possess them — e.g., a man is possessed by a desire for alcohol or sex or what have you and does not possess them by ruling them according to reason. Concupiscence makes man ashamed of his own body. "More exactly," John Paul says, "he has shame not so much of the body, but more precisely of concupiscence: *he has shame of the body motivated by concupiscence.*" He goes on to say in a passage that should be of particular interest to psychologists:

> He has shame of the body motivated by that state of his spirit to which theology and psychology give the name: desire or concupiscence, although with a meaning that is not entirely the same. The biblical and theological meaning of desire and concupiscence differs from the one used in psychology. For psychology, desire springs from a lack or necessity, which the desired value must appease. Biblical concupiscence, as we deduce from 1 John 2:16, indicates *the state of the human spirit distanced from original simplicity and from the fullness of values* that man and the world possess "in the dimensions of God." This simplicity and fullness of the value of the human body in the first experience of its masculinity/femininity, about which Genesis 2:23–25 speaks later underwent a radical transformation "in the dimensions of the world." And at that point, together with the concupiscence of the body, shame was born. (28.5, pp. 245–246)

Shame has a double meaning: "it indicates the threat to the value and at the same time it preserves this value in an interior way" (28.6). Shame is experienced because a human being fears the sexual values of his body will be consumed by the lust of others, and he thus seeks to protect those values because they are *personal.*

Turning his attention to concupiscence, the Holy Father shows how it menaces the "communion of persons" and distorts the spousal meaning of the body. Since the body, after the fall, no longer expresses the person adequately, "the original power of communicating themselves to each other, about which Genesis 2:25 speaks, has been shattered" (29.2, p. 247). To sum matters up:

> "That which is in the world," *namely concupiscence*, brings with it an almost constitutive *difficulty in identifying oneself with one's own body*, not only in the sphere of one's own subjectivity, but even more so *in regard to the subjectivity of the other human being*, of woman for man and man for woman. (29.4, p. 249)

Because of concupiscence the man will want to "dominate" the woman and the woman, who will desire her husband (cf. Gen 3:16), will feel a lack of full unity. Thus the *"original beatifying conjugal union of persons was to be deformed in man's heart by concupiscence"* (30.4, p. 251). An adequate analysis of Genesis 3, the Pope maintains, "leads thus to the conclusion that the threefold concupiscence [referred to in John 2:16–17], including that of the body, brings with it a limitation of the spousal meaning of the body itself, the spousal meaning in which man and woman shared in the state of original innocence" (31.5, p. 255). Nonetheless, the human body, independently of our states of consciousness and our experiences, retains its spousal meaning (cf. 30.5).

"Looking to Desire," and Adultery in the Heart

In the Sermon on the Mount, Jesus deepens the meaning of "Do not commit adultery" by revealing the ethical meaning of the commandment (36.1, p. 271). Christ speaks of "adultery in the heart." If the fundamental meaning of adultery is that of a sin of the body, how can what a man does in his heart also count as adultery? "The man about whom Christ speaks

in the Sermon on the Mount — the man who looks 'to desire'
— is without doubt the man of concupiscence" (38.2, p. 279).
But to see why he must be regarded as committing adultery,
we must recognize the ethical and anthropological significance
of the "look to desire" or "lustful look."

"The look," the Holy Father says,

> *expresses what is in the heart.* The look, I would say, expresses
> man as a whole. If one assumes in general that man "acts in
> conformity with what he is": (*operari sequitur esse*) [operation
> follows being], in the present case Christ wants to show that
> man "looks" in conformity with what he is: (*intueri sequitur
> esse*) [looking follows being]. (39.4, p. 285)

Continuing, he says:

> [Lustful] "desiring," "looking to desire," indicates an experi-
> ence of the value of the body in which its spousal meaning
> ceases to be spousal precisely because of concupiscence. What
> also ceases is its procreative meaning.... So then, when man
> "desires" and "looks to desire"... he *experiences* more or less
> explicitly *the detachment from that meaning of the body* which
> ... stands at the basis of the communion of persons: both out-
> side of marriage and — in a particular way — when man and
> woman are called to build the union "in the body." (39.5, pp.
> 285–286)

In further analyzing concupiscent desire, John Paul characterizes it as deceiving the human heart with respect to the
perennial call to man and woman to "give" themselves and
establish a communion of persons, a call revealed in the mystery of creation and mediated by the body. Thus concupiscent
desire, as a "realization of the concupiscence of the flesh ...
diminishes the meaning of ... this invitation" (40.1–2, p. 287).
Concupiscent desire is thus, he continues, "an *intentional
reduction*, a restriction, as it were, or closure of the horizon of

the mind and the heart." It leads one to ignore the value of the person as person, a being to be loved, and focuses on the person's *sexual values* as the only real values and "fitting object of the satisfaction of one's own sexuality" (40.3, pp. 287–288).

From this it follows that although society does not regard the exterior act of genital union between a married man and his own wife as "adultery" (42.5, p. 295),

> we conclude that ... in *understanding* "adultery in the heart," Christ takes into consideration not only the real juridical state of life of the man and the woman in question. Christ makes the moral evaluation of "desire" depend above all *on the personal dignity of the man and the woman*; and this is important both in the case of unmarried persons and — perhaps even more so — in the case of spouses, husband and wife. (42.7, p. 296; see 43.1, p. 297)

The Holy Father then concludes: "'Adultery in the heart' is not committed only because man 'looks' in this way at a woman who is not his wife, but *precisely because he looks in this way at a woman.* Even if he were to look in this way at the woman who is his wife, he would commit the same adultery 'in the heart'" (43.2, p. 298).

The Holy Father's comment here was met with some hostile reaction because it was not understood. However, his meaning recaptures the authentic teaching of the Fathers of the Church and Saint Thomas Aquinas. The Pope is referring to a husband who is so possessed by a desire for sexual pleasure that he forces himself on his wife even if she has a good reason not to engage in the conjugal act. Such a husband is not acting in a loving way. He makes the act to be something that is not truly conjugal — it is not open to the unitive good but rather he intentionally sets it aside and makes the act truly one of adultery.

Reaffirming the Goodness of the Body

In TOB 44–45, the Pope rejects a Manichaean repudiation of the "body" and any interpretation of Christ's Sermon on the Mount (e.g., of the verses in which Christ speaks of "tearing out your eye" or "cutting off your hand" in Matthew 5:29–30 [cf. 44.5–6, pp. 303–305]) that would denigrate the value of the body. Indeed, *the judgment about the concupiscence of the flesh has thus a meaning essentially different from the one that Manichaean ontology is able to presuppose* (45.1, p. 306). What Christ condemns is a lustful heart. A desire for the "body" is not itself sinful desire, for the body itself is good. Thus John Paul II reaffirms that the body, in its masculinity and femininity, is called to manifest the person, to manifest the spirit, and to do so particularly by means of the conjugal union of husband and wife when they unite to form "one flesh." Christ defends this meaning of the body, its "sacramental" significance. Christ's "redemption of the body" "does not … indicate ontological evil as a constituent attribute of the human body, but points only to *man's sinfulness*, by which *he lost*, among other things, *the clear sense of the spousal meaning of the body*, in which the interior dominion and freedom of the spirit expresses itself" (45.2, p. 307).

Redeeming the Body

After criticizing views of Nietzsche, Marx, and Freud that in some measure identify the meaning of concupiscence but do so inadequately, the Pope insists we must go further. Christ's words in Matthew 5:27–28

> do not allow us to stop at the accusation of the human heart
> and to cast it into a state of continual suspicion, but … they
> must be understood and interpreted as an appeal addressed

to the heart.... Redemption is a truth, a reality, in the name of which man must feel himself called ... *to rediscover*, or even better, to realize, the spousal meaning of the body and to express in this way the interior freedom of the gift, that is, the freedom of that spiritual state and power that derive from mastery over the concupiscence of the flesh. (46.4, pp. 312–313)

Christ's words "testify that *the original power* (and thus also the grace) *of the mystery of creation becomes* for each of them [man and woman] *the power* (that is, the grace) *of the mystery of redemption*. This concerns the very 'nature,' the very substrate of the humanity of the person, the deepest impulses of the 'heart'" (46.5, p. 313; cf. 46.6).

"Eros" must not be confused with lustful concupiscence. For Plato it "represents the inner power that draws man toward all that is good, true, and beautiful" (47.2, p. 316). It refers also to the natural and hence "good" desire experienced in the attraction of men for women and vice versa. However "erotic" desire is often identified with concupiscent desire or lust. The Pope, after noting the many semantic understandings of "eros," says:

It seems in fact possible that in the sphere of the concept of "eros" — keeping its Platonic meaning in mind — one can find room for that ethos, for those ethical and indirectly also theological contents that have been drawn in the course of our analyses from Christ's appeal to the human heart in the Sermon on the Mount. (47.4, p. 317)

In other words, "erotic" love is *not* "pornography" or love of the flesh; it is rather a valid form of love and was so regarded by philosophers such as Plato, a form of love *open to "ethos" or right reason.*

While the words of Matthew 5:27–28 are an "accusation" of the human heart, they are at the same time and even more so an appeal addressed to it. This appeal is the category proper to the ethos of redemption. The call to what is true, good, and beautiful means at the same time, in the ethos of redemption, the necessity of overcoming what derives from the threefold concupiscence. It means also *the possibility and the necessity of transforming* what has been weighed down by the concupiscence of the flesh. Further, if the words of Matthew 5:27–28 represent such a call, then this means that in the erotic sphere, "eros" and "ethos" do not diverge, are not opposed to each other, but *are called to meet in the human heart, and to bear fruit in this meeting.* (47.5, p. 318)

Ethos must become the "constituent form" of eros. Ethos is in no way hostile to "spontaneity." The person who accepts the ethos of Matthew 5:27–28 "should know that he or she is also called *to full and mature spontaneity* in relationships that are born from the perennial attraction of masculinity and femininity. Such spontaneity is itself the gradual fruit of the discernment of the impulses of one's own heart" (48.2, p. 319). "The discernment we are speaking about is by its essence related to spontaneity.... [A] noble pleasure is one thing, [mere] sexual desire another; when sexual desire is connected with a noble pleasure, it differs from desire pure and simple" (48.4, p. 320).

There cannot be such spontaneity in all the movements and impulses that spring from mere carnal concupiscence.... At the price of mastery over these impulses, man reaches that *deeper and more mature spontaneity* with which his "heart," by mastering these impulses, rediscovers the spiritual beauty of the sign constituted by the human body in its masculinity and femininity. (48.5, p. 321)

To put this another way, *"self-mastery," an essential ingredient of purity of heart, enables us to take possession of our desires and not be possessed by them, precisely so that we can give ourselves away in love.*

Redemption

In the first of the final two audiences of this part of TOB, John Paul II notes that in Matthew 5:27–28 and "also in the Sermon on the Mount *Christ speaks in the perspective of the redemption* of man and the world (and thus precisely of the 'redemption of the body'). This is, in fact, the perspective of the whole gospel, of the whole teaching, even more, of the whole mission of Christ" (49.3, p. 323). In his sermon, Jesus does not invite man to return to the state of original innocence, because this has been irretrievably lost,

> but *he calls him to find* — on the foundation of the perennial and ... indestructible meanings of what is "human" — *the living forms of the "new man."* In this way a connection is formed, even a continuity, between the "beginning" and the perspective of redemption. In the ethos of the redemption of the body, the original ethos of creation was to be taken up anew. (49.4, p. 323)

In the second audience, the Holy Father seeks to analyze and clarify the meaning of purity of heart. In contrast to Old Testament laws regarding "cleanliness" or "purity" in that sense, Christ took care "against connecting purity in the moral (ethical) sense with physiology and the organic processes in quesion" (50.3, p. 328). By citing the words of Matthew 15:18–20 ("... out of the heart come evil intentions, murder, adultery.... These make a man unclean"), Christ

> speaks *about every moral evil*, every sin.... [I]t follows that the concept of "purity" and of "impurity" in the moral sense is a rather general concept, not a specific one: thus every moral good is a manifestation of purity and every moral evil a manifestation of impurity. (50.4, p. 328)

The Teaching of Saint Paul

TOB 51–57 take up the teaching of Saint Paul. TOB 58 and 59 in a way recapitulate the themes of the entire second cycle, and TOB 60–63 concern the body in art. I will omit consideration of 60–63, which is an appendix to this cycle.

"Flesh" Versus "Spirit" and Justification by Faith (See Especially Galatians and Romans)

The Pope analyzes Paul's words in Galatians 5:17, "the flesh has desires contrary to the Spirit, and the Spirit has desires contrary to the flesh." For Paul the "flesh" indicates *not only the 'outer' man, but also the man 'interiorly' subjected to the 'world'"* (51.1, pp. 330–331), i.e., the Johannine world wounded by sin, not the world God created. The desires of the man subject to concupiscence are a "manifestation of life 'according to the flesh'" as opposed to "life 'according to the Spirit.'" "This man lives, as it were, at the pole opposite to what 'the Spirit wants'" (51.2, p. 332). This opposition between what the "flesh" and the "Spirit" want in historical man, prominent in Paul's letters to the Galatians and Romans "is set in the context of the Pauline teaching about *justification* by faith, that is, by *the power of Christ* himself *working in man's innermost [being] through the Holy Spirit*" (51.3, p. 332).

Paul's horizons are the "beginning" in the sense of the first sin from which "life according to the flesh" originated the one horizon, while the final victory over death is the second horizon. The "justification" we have through faith in Christ "does not constitute simply a dimension of the divine plan of salvation and of man's sanctification, but according to St. Paul it is *a real power at work in man that reveals and affirms itself in his actions*" (51.4, p. 333). After then contrasting the "works of the flesh" (e.g., fornication, enmity, anger) and those "of the

Spirit" (e.g., love, joy, peace, self-control) (cf. Gal 5:19–21), the Pope concludes by saying that "behind each of these realizations [i.e., the "works of the Spirit"], these forms of behavior, these moral virtues, stands a *specific choice*, that is, an effort of the will, *a fruit of the human spirit* permeated by the Spirit of God, which manifests itself in choosing the good." Among the fruits of the Spirit Saint Paul includes *"self-mastery"* (51.6, pp. 334–335), and John Paul II will return to this issue in TOB 53. But in 52 he stresses that

> when Paul speaks about the necessity of putting to death deeds of the body with the Spirit's help, he expresses precisely what Christ spoke about in the Sermon on the Mount when he appealed to the human heart and exhorted it to mastery over desires, including those that express themselves in a man's "look" directed toward a woman with the purpose of satisfying the concupiscence of the flesh. Such *mastery*, or, as Paul writes, *"putting to death the deeds of the body by the Spirit," is an indispensable condition of "life according to the Spirit,"* that is, of the "life" that is the antithesis of the "death" about which he speaks in the same context. Life "according to the flesh" bears fruit, in fact, in "death," that is, it brings with it the "death" according to the Spirit. "The term 'death,' therefore, does not signify only bodily death, but also the sin that theology was to call mortal." (52.4, p. 337)

True Freedom, Self-control, and "Purity"

In Galatians Paul emphasizes the "ethical subordination of freedom to that element in which the whole law is fulfilled, namely, love" (53.2, p. 339).

> The one who *lives* in this way, *"according to the flesh"*, that is, who subjects himself — even if not altogether consciously, nevertheless effectively — to the threefold concupiscence, particularly to the concupiscence of the flesh, *ceases to be*

capable of this freedom for which "Christ has set us free"; he also ceases to be suitable *for the true gift* of self, which is the fruit and expression of such freedom. He further ceases to be capable of the gift organically linked with the spousal meaning of the human body. (53.3, p. 340)

Paul helps us to see Christian and evangelical "purity of heart" in a wider perspective, linking it "with love, in which 'the whole law finds its fullness'" (53.4). In his list of the works of the Spirit, Paul does not list "purity." He only mentions *"self-mastery,"* Greek *enkrateia* (Gal 5.22). One can recognize this "mastery" as a virtue that concerns continence in the area of all the desires of the senses, above all in the sexual sphere. However, for Paul purity did not require complete abstinence from sexual life.

The Sanctity of the Human Body and Respect for It

In 1 Thessalonians 4:3–5 Paul writes: "…this is the will of God, your sanctification: that you abstain from unchastity, that each one of you knows how to keep his own body in holiness and reverence, not as the object of lustful passions." He continues, in verses 4:7–8: "God did not call us to impurity but to sanctification. Therefore, whoever rejects these norms rejects not a man but God, who gives his Holy Spirit to you." A man manifests the self-control, the "purity" that Paul demands, when "he knows how to keep his own body in holiness and reverence, not as the object of lustful passions" (54.2, p. 342). Purity requires both "abstention" (from unchaste behavior) and "mastery" over "lustful passions" (54.3, p. 343). The Pope then makes a *very important point*, relating the Pauline meaning of "honor" to his teaching on purity:

In order to understand the Pauline teaching about purity, one must enter deeply into the meaning of the term "reverence," obviously understood here as a power belonging to the spiritual order ... this interior power ... gives full dimension to purity as a virtue, that is, as an ability to act in that whole sphere in which man discovers, in his own innermost [being], the many impulses of "lustful passions" and at times, for various reasons, surrenders to them. (54.4, p. 344)

John Paul II affirms that Paul's teaching on respect for the sanctity of the human body, central to the Thessalonians text, is deepened by what Paul says in 1 Corinthians 12:18, 22–25) (cited in 54.5, p. 344). In this text, Paul uses the analogy of the human body in explaining the various roles of the members of the Church.

Commenting on this text, the Pope says:

Although the topic of the text just quoted is the theology of the Church as the Body of Christ, one can nevertheless note in the margin of this passage that with his great ecclesiological analogy ... Paul contributes at the same time to *a deeper understanding of the theology of the body*. While in 1 Thessalonians he writes about keeping the body "with holiness and reverence," in the passage ... from 1 Corinthians he wishes to show this human body as deserving reverence or respect; one could also say that he wants to teach the recipients of his letter the right understanding of the human body. Thus, this Pauline description of the human body in 1 Corinthians seems to be strictly tied to the recommendations of 1 Thessalonians.... This is an important line of thought, perhaps the essential one of the Pauline teaching on purity. (54.6, pp. 344–345)

Saint Paul's Description of the Body, His Teaching on Purity, and the Phenomenon of "Shame"

The Pauline description of the human body in the text from 1 Corinthians referred to above is not "scientific." But:

[W]hat shapes its specific character, what particularly justifies its presence in Sacred Scripture, is precisely this evaluation [of the human body] woven into the description and expressed in its "narrative-realistic" plot. One can certainly say that *this description would not be possible without the whole truth of creation*; nor without the truth of the *"redemption of the body."* [T]he Pauline description of the body *corresponds precisely to the* spiritual *attitude of "reverence"* for the human body that is due to the "holiness" (see 1 Thess 4:3–5, 7–8) that wells up from the mysteries of creation and redemption. (55.3, p. 346)

In a remarkable passage, John Paul then links all these things to the phenomenon of *shame*. He writes:

In Paul's expressions about "unpresentable members" of the human body, as well as about those that "seem to be weaker" or those "that we think less honorable," we find, it seems to us, *the testimony of the same shame* that the first human beings, male and female, had experienced after original sin. This shame impressed itself on them and on all generations of "historical" man as the fruit of the threefold concupiscence with particular reference to the concupiscence of the flesh. And what impressed itself at the same time … is a certain "echo" of the same original innocence of man: a photographic "negative," as it were, the "positive" of which was precisely original innocence" (55.4, pp. 346–347).… This same shame seems to be at the same time the basis of what the Apostle says in 1 Corinthians: "Those members of the body that we think less honorable we clothe with greater reverence, and our unpresentable members are treated with greater modesty" (1 Cor 12:23). Thus, one can say that *from shame is born "reverence"* for one's own body, a reverence that Paul asks us to keep (1 Thess 4:4). (55.5, p. 347)

In other words, because of shame experienced when our private parts evoke concupiscent desire in others, we show that they are in truth honorable and ought to be reverenced as truly integral to our being by modestly clothing them.

Saint Paul links his description of the human body with the state of "historical" man, at whose threshold in history there is the experience of shame connected with "discord in the body." But Saint Paul "also indicates *the way that* leads (precisely on the basis of the sense of shame) to the transformation of this [historical] state, to the *gradual victory over this 'disunion in the body'*, a victory that can and should be realized in the human heart. This is precisely the road of purity" (55.7, p. 348).

The Supernatural Holiness of the Body; the "Profaning" Character of Sexual Sin

For Paul, purity has both a moral dimension as a virtue and a charismatic dimension as a gift, a fruit of life "according to the Spirit" (56.1). In 1 Corinthians 6:19 Paul writes: "Or do you not know that your body is a temple of the Holy Spirit within you, which you have from God, and that you do not belong to yourselves?" He says this only after warning the Corinthians about the grave moral requirements of purity: "Flee from prostitution! Any sin that a man commits is outside his body; but the one who gives himself to fornication sins against his own body" (1 Cor 6:18). Such sins therefore "profane" the body, depriving a man's or woman's body of the honor and reverence due it because of the dignity of the person. John Paul goes on to say:

> [T]he Apostle, however, goes further: according to him, a sin against the body is also a *"profaning of the temple."* What is decisive for the dignity of the human body, in Paul's eyes, is not only the human spirit, thanks to which man is constituted as a personal subject, but [also] much more so the super-

natural reality of the indwelling and continuous presence of the Holy Spirit in man — in his soul and body — as the fruit of the redemption accomplished by Christ. (56.3, p. 350)

Moreover, our redemption came at a price, that of Christ's death (1 Cor 6:20).

The fact that in Jesus Christ the human body became the body of the God-Man has the effect of a new supernatural elevation in every human being, which every Christian must take into account in his behavior toward "his own" body and obviously also toward another's body: man toward woman and woman toward man. *The redemption of the body* brings with it the establishment in Christ and for Christ a new *measure of the holiness of the body.* (56.4, p. 351)

Thus in 1 Corinthians 6:15–17 Paul makes it clear that a Christian, who has become one body with Christ, not only commits an immoral sexual act by joining his body to a prostitute but also profanes the whole body of Christ. Because the human body, redeemed by Christ, is so supernaturally holy, Christians have a special duty to "keep" their bodies "in holiness and reverence" (56.5, p. 351).

Summing up Paul's Teaching on Purity

John Paul cites 1 Corinthians 6:20, the end of Paul's argument that sexual sin by a Christian profanes the entire body of Christ: "Therefore glorify God in your body." He then sums up:

Purity as a virtue or ability of "keeping one's own body with holiness and reverence," allied with the gift of piety as a fruit of the Holy Spirit's dwelling in the "temple" of the body, causes in the body such a fullness of dignity in interpersonal relations that *God himself is thereby glorified.* Purity is the glory of the human body before God. It is the glory of God in the human body, through which masculinity and femininity are manifested. From purity springs that singular beauty that permeates every sphere of reciprocal common life between human beings and allows them to express in it the simplicity and depth, the cordiality and unrepeatable authenticity of personal trust. (57.3, p. 353)

The Pope then links Paul's thought to the notion set forth in the Wisdom literature of the Old Testament (see Sir 23:4–6, 51:20, Wis 8:21) that "it is not so much *purity that is a condition for wisdom*, but *wisdom that is a condition for purity as a particular gift of God*. It seems that already in the Wisdom texts just quoted the twofold meaning of purity takes shape: as virtue and as gift" (57.4, p. 354). Thus:

[W]hat seems to be fundamental for the Pauline understanding of purity ... is *the anthropology of rebirth in the Holy Spirit* (cf. Jn 3:5ff.). This anthropology grows from roots that plunge down into the reality of the redemption of the body achieved by Christ, a redemption whose final expression is the resurrection. There are deep reasons for linking the whole topic of purity with the words of the Gospel in which Jesus appeals to the resurrection. [This will be the next stage of our considerations (see TOB 64–85).] (57.5, pp. 354–355)

Summing Up

In TOB 58 John Paul begins by reviewing "the beginning" (the Genesis texts), the contrast among the "state of innocence" and "the state of sin" and "historical" man, the one subject to concupiscence, the meaning of concupiscence, and so forth (58.2–3). He then focuses on the "truth" about man and his vocation rooted in the narrative of the "beginning" to which Christ appealed. This truth, he affirms, is a *truth of an ethical character* ... [it is also] a normative truth, as normative as the truth contained in the commandment "You shall not commit adultery." Christ's interpretation of this commandment indicates the evil that must be avoided and defeated — the evil of the concupiscence of the flesh — and at the same time it points out the good for which the way is opened by overcoming [reductive] desires. This good is the "purity of heart" about which Christ speaks in the same context of the Sermon on the Mount. From the biblical point of view, "purity of heart" signifies being free from *every kind* of sin or guilt, not only from sins that concern the "concupiscence of the flesh." (58.4, p. 357)

This explanation is most important for seeing how "purity of heart" in TOB differs from the more limited understanding of such purity in theological literature focusing on that purity vis-à-vis sexual issues. In other words, for Paul "purity of heart" means a heart free from the threefold concupiscence of the flesh, of the eyes, and of the pride of life found in the Johannine literature.

The truth, valid for all men, contained in Christ's words is "*not only an ethical truth, but also* the essential truth about man, *the anthropological truth*. This is precisely the reason why we return to these words in formulating the theology of the body" (58.5, p. 358). Christ's words are realistic, and they do not try to make the human heart return to the state of innocence, insofar as this has been irremediably lost. But they show man

the path toward a purity of heart that is possible and accessible for him even in the state of hereditary sinfulness. It is the purity of the "man of concupiscence," who is nevertheless inspired by the word of the Gospel and open to "life according to the Spirit" ... that is, the purity of the man of concupiscence who is completely enveloped by the "redemption of the body" achieved by Christ.... The normative meaning of Christ's words is deeply rooted in their anthropological meaning, in the dimension of human interiority. (58.5, p. 358)

This shows us that historical man can recover and live the "spousal" meaning of the body precisely because of Christ's redemptive act and man's union with the redeeming Christ.

The evangelical meaning of purity developed by Paul

opens the way toward an ever more perfect discovery of the dignity of the human body, which is organically connected with the freedom of the gift of the person in the integral authenticity of its personal subjectivity, male or female. In this way, *purity, in the sense of temperance* matures in the heart of the human being who cultivates it and who *seeks to discover and affirm the spousal meaning of the body* in its integral truth. (58.6, p. 359)

Concluding this number, John Paul II writes:

In mature purity, man enjoys the fruits of victory over concupiscence, a victory about which St. Paul writes when he exhorts everyone to "keep his own body in holiness and reverence" (1 Thess 4:4). Even more, such maturity partly shows the efficaciousness of the gift of the Holy Spirit, whose "temple" the human body is (see 1 Cor 6:19). This gift is above all that of piety (*"donum pietatis"*) which gives back to the experience of the body — especially in the case of the sphere of reciprocal relations between man and woman — all *its simplicity, its lucid clarity*, and also *its interior joy.* (58.7, p. 359)

The final audience (59) in many ways sums matters up. In it, the Pope refers in particular to *Gaudium et Spes*, 47–52 (devoted to fostering marriage and its dignity), and Paul VI's encyclical *Humanae Vitae*. He emphasizes that the teaching of the Church's magisterium on marriage and sexual morality is intended to apply Christ's words to situations today. It serves as a pedagogy whose purpose is to show that "affective mani-festations," especially those "proper to conjugal life," must be and can be, precisely because of Christ's redemptive act, in conformity with the dignity of the human person (see espe-cially 59.6–7).

4. The Fulfillment of Marriage and the Spousal Meaning of the Body in the Resurrection (TOB 64–86; Part 1, Chapter 3)

Here I will sketch the major ideas in these audiences by focusing on two areas:

1. TOB 64–69: These talks are devoted to an analysis of the synoptic accounts of Jesus' dialogue with the Sadducees regarding the resurrection in Matthew 22:24–30, Mark 12:18–20, and Luke 20:27–40.

2. TOB 70–72: These talks take up Saint Paul's interpre-tation of the resurrection in 1 Corinthians 15:4–49.

I will omit detailed consideration of TOB 73–86, which are concerned with continence for the kingdom. In them the Holy Father shows that another way in addition to marriage is open to Christians to fulfill their vocation to love and to respect the spousal meaning of the body. This is the call to a life of conse-crated celibacy, the value of which in no way disparages mar-riage and, in truth, is meaningful only in the light of marriage while at the same time deepening our understanding of mar-riage. At times marriage itself may require complete conti-nence if necessary to protect the spousal meaning of the body — for instance if, after the marriage had been duly consum-mated by the conjugal act, one spouse were injured in such a way that he/she could not unite in the conjugal act.

The Dialogue with the Sadducees

John Paul regards Christ's dialogue with the Sadducees as reported in the Synoptics as *"the third component of the triptych"* of Christ's own statements constituting the theology of the body. The other two parts are the dialogue with the Pharisees about divorce, and the Sermon on the Mount and the man of concupiscence. In his dialogue with the Sadducees, "Jesus appeals to the resurrection, thereby revealing a completely new dimension of the mystery of man" (64.1, p. 380). Later the Pope writes that when Christ says: "When they rise from the dead, they take neither wife nor husband" (Mk 12:25) he speaks words *"which have a key meaning for the theology of the body"* (66.1, p. 387). Jesus makes it clear that marriage "belongs *exclusively 'to this world.'"* (66.2) But these same words "seem to affirm, at one and the same time, that human bodies ... will preserve their specific masculine or feminine character and that *the meaning of being male or female in the body* will be *constituted and understood differently* in the "other world" (66.4, p. 388). We need to recall that "the truth about the resurrection had a *key meaning for the formation of theological anthropology as a whole,* which could simply be considered *'anthropology of the resurrection'"* (66.6, p. 390). In the resurrection the human body will be "spiritualized" and indeed "divinized" (see 67.1–3, pp. 391–393).

TOB 69.3–4 are of great help in understanding this. In 69.3 the Pope notes that although Christ points out that man's identity will be realized differently in the eschatological experience of the resurrection than it was in the "beginning," man nevertheless "will always be the same" (p. 398). An important passage in 69.4 affirms:

> *the original* and fundamental *meaning of being a body*...precisely that "spousal" meaning — *is united to the fact that man is*

created as a person and is called to a life "in communione person-arum." ... Marriage and procreation only give concrete reality to that meaning in the dimensions of history. The resurrection indicates the closure of the historical dimension ... but [Christ's words] allow us also to deduce that the "spousal" meaning of the body in the resurrection to the future life will perfectly correspond both to the fact that man as male-female is a person, created in the "image and likeness of God," and to the fact that this image is realized in the communion of persons. That "spousal" meaning of being a body will, therefore, be realized as a *meaning that is perfectly personal and communitarian at the same time.* (p. 399)

The resurrected body is a *human* body, with its *spousal* meaning — its masculinity and femininity — fully present, perfected, *spiritualized*, and *divinized*. In short, the spousal meaning of the body is not something of significance only in this life. Our bodies always have this spousal meaning, just as the human body of Jesus had a spousal meaning that was fulfilled and perfected in his resurrection from the dead. He is the "first fruit" of his own redemption, and he is now the kind of being we will become in our resurrected bodies, the spousal significance of which will be redeemed and fulfilled.

Saint Paul in 1 Corinthians 15

The Pope notes that:

Between the answer given to the Sadducees ... and Paul's apostolate, the event that took place first of all was Christ's own resurrection and a series of encounters with the Risen One, among which one should number as the last link in the chain of the event that occurred near Damascus. Saul or Paul of Tarsus ... had *his own post-paschal experience.* ... At the basis of his faith in the resurrection, which he expresses above all in 1 Corinthians 15, certainly stands that encounter with the Risen One. (70.1, p. 402)

Thus

the resurrection of Christ is the final and fullest word *of the self-revelation* of the living God as *"God ... of the living"* (Mk 12:27).... The resurrection is also the answer given by the God of life to the historical inevitability of death, to which man was subjected after breaking the first covenant and which entered his history together with sin. First Corinthians 15 illustrates this answer about the victory won over death with extraordinary clear-sightedness by a presentation of the resurrection of Christ as the beginning of that eschatological fulfillment in which through him and in him everything will return to the Father, everything will be subjected to him.... And so ... death is vanquished as well; "the last enemy to be destroyed will be death" (1 Cor 15:26). (70.3, pp. 402–403)

Paul's anthropology of the resurrection is consistent with the anthropology emerging from the synoptic account of the dialogue with the Sadducees. But the Pope maintains that Paul's position is more developed. His text shows that "the *eschatological perspective* on man, based on faith in the 'resurrection of the body,' *is united with the reference to the 'beginning'* as well as the deep consciousness *of man's 'historical' situation"* (70.5, p. 404).

In his synthesis Paul "*reproduces* everything *Christ had proclaimed"* in the triptych of Christ's dialogues (see 70.6, p. 404). The Pope links Romans 8:19–23, where Paul writes of all creation as groaning and suffering labor pains, and waiting with eager longing for the revelation of the sons of God and the redemption of the body, with 1 Corinthians 15 (see 70.7–8, pp. 404–405). The Pope also links Paul's contrast of the first man (Adam), who consists of earth, with the second man (Christ), who comes from heaven (71.1–2, p. 406). He argues that the

> "heavenly man" — the man of the resurrection — ... is the fulfillment and confirmation of what corresponds to the psychosomatic constitution of humanity ... in the thought and plan of the one who created man from the beginning in his image and likeness. The humanity of the "first Adam," the "man of earth," carries within itself ... *a particular potentiality ... for receiving* all *that the "second Adam" became*, the heavenly Man, namely, Christ: what he became in his resurrection. It is the same humanity, which all human beings, sons of the first Adam, participate in. It is "perishable" — since it is fleshly — while being burdened with the heritage of sin, and yet it carries in itself at the same time the potentiality of "incorruptibility." (71.3, p. 407)

Although Saint Paul speaks of "the body" and not "human nature" or "humanity," we can, the Pope maintains, conclude in view of both the proximate and remote contexts of his writing

> that what is at issue for him is not only the body, but the whole man in his bodiliness, therefore also in his ontological complexity. Without any doubt, if in the whole visible world (cosmos) only this body, which is *the* human *body*, carries in itself "the potentiality of the resurrection" ... the reason is that, persisting from the beginning in the psychosomatic unity of its personal being, *it can gather and reproduce in this "earthly" image and likeness of God also the "heavenly" image of* the last Adam, *Christ*. The Pauline anthropology of the resurrection is cosmic and universal. (70.4, p. 407)

In fact, toward the conclusion of his analyses of 1 Corinthians 15 and Romans 8:19–23, John Paul II writes:

One can, therefore, say that we are dealing with the anthropology of the resurrection not only in 1 Corinthians 15, but that St. Paul's entire anthropology (and ethics) are permeated by the mystery of the resurrection, by which we have definitively received the Holy Spirit. First Corinthians 15 constitutes the Pauline interpretation of the "other world" and of man's state in that world, in which, with the resurrection of the body, everyone will share fully in the gift of the life-giving Spirit, that is, in the fruit of Christ's resurrection. (72.6, p. 411)

Thus it follows that in the resurrected, spiritualized, and divinized human body its *spousal meaning* will be fully manifest and glorified in the *communio personarum* of all those human beings, men and women, whose masculinity and femininity will be, in union with the Risen Lord, fully made perfect and an efficacious sign of the triune God's own nuptial mystery.

5. The Function of the Spousal Meaning of the Body in the Sacrament (TOB 87– 133; Part 2, Chapters 1, 2, and 3)

Part 2, "The Sacrament," is divided into three chapters:

1. Chapter 1 (TOB 87–102): "The Dimension of Covenant and of Grace." In this chapter, the Holy Father considers the sacrament of Marriage from the aspect of *grace and covenant.*

2. Chapter 2 (TOB 103–117): "The Dimension of Sign." Here, John Paul II takes up the function of the spousal meaning of the body in the sacrament and in the "language of the body." The Pope deals with this subject especially in the first two sections of this chapter — "'Language of the Body' and the

Reality of the Sign" (103–107), and "The Song of Songs" (108–113). The third section, "When the 'Language of the Body' becomes the Language of the Liturgy" (114–117), focuses on the subject indicated by its title. This complements the first two sections of chapter 2, in which the Pope shows that the "language of the body" must be reread in light of the prophetic tradition (Hosea, Ezekiel, Deutero-Isaiah, and others) and of the Song of Songs. I will focus on audiences 103–113.

3. Chapter 3 (TOB 118–133): "He Gave Them the Law of Life as Their Inheritance." In this chapter, the Pope shows how the theology of the body is central to understanding Paul VI's teaching in *Humanae Vitae*.

In the following material, I do not take up chapter 1 of part 2, "The Dimension of Covenant and of Grace." Some of the themes overlap with other material covered in this book. It can be summed up as follows: in essence it is a masterful exegesis of the text in Ephesians 5 on marriage as the "great mystery" of Christ's bridal union with his Church. John Paul discusses the sacramentality of Christian marriage as a true sacrament of the new law. This sacrament not only points to but efficaciously shares in that love-giving, life-giving, and grace-giving reality.

The Dimension of Sign

In the first audience of chapter 2, "'Language of the Body' and the Reality of the Sign" (TOB 103), John Paul clearly identifies his subject matter:

> Given that the sacrament is the sign by means of which the saving reality of grace and the covenant is expressed and realized, we must now consider it under the aspect of sign, while the preceding reflections were devoted to the reality of grace and the covenant. (103.3, p. 532)

The Holy Father begins by affirming that marriage comes into being by means of the word, when the man and the woman *consent* to take each other as husband and wife. But these words "can only be fulfilled by the *copula conjugale* (conjugal intercourse). This reality (the *copula conjugale*), moreover, has been defined from the very beginning by institution of the Creator. 'A man will leave his father and his mother and unite with his wife, and the two will be one flesh' (Gen 2:24)" (103.2, p. 532). Continuing, he says:

> The words, "I take you as my wife/as my husband," bear within themselves precisely that perennial and ever unique and unrepeatable "language of the body," and they place it at the same time in the context of the communion of persons.... In this way the perennial and ever new "language of the body" *is not only the "substratum," but in some sense also the constitutive content of the communion of persons.* The persons — the man and the woman — become a reciprocal gift for each other. They become this gift in their masculinity and femininity while they discover the spousal meaning of the body and refer it reciprocally to themselves in an irreversible way: in the dimension of life as a whole. (103.5, p. 533)

If we now reread the "language of the body" in light of the prophetic tradition begun by Hosea and continued by Ezekiel and others, we discover that the human body speaks a "language" whose "*author is man*, as male or female, as bridegroom or bride: man with his perennial vocation to the communion of persons." But, and this is most important,

> man is *in some sense unable to express* this singular language of his personal existence and vocation *without the body.* He is constituted in such a way from the "beginning" that the deepest words of the spirit — words of love, gift, and faithfulness — call for an appropriate "language of the body." And

without this language, they cannot be fully expressed. (104.7, p. 537)

From this an ethical conclusion follows: In speaking the "language of the body" in truth, one must never violate its spousal meaning, its meaning as "gift." Thus the prophets testified to conjugal chastity and fidelity as the "truth" and to adultery as falsity in the "language of the body" (cf. 104.9, p. 538). The body speaks lies "through all that negates conjugal love, faithfulness, and integrity" (TOB 105.1, pp. 538–539). We all speak of "body language," and the human body speaks lies when it takes rather than gives — e.g., fornicators and live-in lovers say they "love one another," but their bodies do not speak the language of selfless giving but rather of selfish taking; they do not "give themselves" through their bodies but rather "lend themselves" just as long as they find their bodily union satisfying. John Paul says that in this way the essential truth of the sign will remain organically linked to the morality of the spouses' marital conduct (see TOB 105.6, p. 541). Through "the whole of the 'language of the body' … the spouses decide to speak to each other as ministers of the sacrament" (TOB 105.6, p. 541). They not only proclaim the truth coming from God, but John Paul also says they proclaim this truth *in God's name*. In constituting the marital sign in the moment of consent and fulfilling it in the moment of consummation, the spouses *"perform an act of prophetic character. They confirm in this way their share in the prophetic mission of the Church"* received from Christ (TOB 105.2, p. 539).

There *"is an organic link between rereading* the integral meaning of the 'language of the body' in the truth and the consequent *use* of that language in conjugal life" (TOB 106.3, p. 543). Spouses "are explicitly called to bear witness — by correctly using the 'language of the body' — to spousal and procreative love, *a testimony worthy of 'true prophets.'* In this consists the true significance and the greatness of conjugal consent in the sacrament of the Church" (TOB 106.4, p. 544). The "greatness" of conjugal consent is precisely its prophetic witness to the "mystery hidden from eternity in God" — the mystery of Trinitarian life and love that flows through the spousal union of Christ with the Church, reaching the concrete lives of men and women within history.

In the light of Christ's words in the Sermon on the Mount we know that the threefold concupiscence — of the eyes, of pride of life, and in particular the concupiscence of the flesh — *"does not destroy the capacity to reread the 'language of the body' in the truth"* (107.3, p. 546). Precisely because the body has been redeemed by Christ, "historical man" is able

> on the basis of the "language of the body" reread in the truth, *to constitute the sacramental sign of* conjugal *love*, faithfulness, and integrity, and this as an *enduring sign....* He is capable of it even as the "man of concupiscence," since he is at the same time "called" by the reality of the redemption of Christ. (107.4, p. 546)

To sum up thus far: we know that through Christ's redeeming death and resurrection we can recover the spousal meaning of the body. This, we shall now see, was anticipated in the Song of Songs.

John Paul thinks that for rereading the "language of the body" in the truth "the Song of Songs has an altogether singular significance" (TOB 113.6, p. 592). The bridegroom rereads this "language" at one and the same time with his heart and with his eyes (TOB 108.8, p. 558). The bridegroom is integrated internally and externally. If a "look" determines the very intentionality of existence, the lover has determined to live in the truth of the *gift*. He respects woman as a gift. His look concentrates "on the whole female 'I' of the bride." He sees her as a *person* — a subject — created for her own sake. And her personhood "speaks to him through every feminine trait, giving rise to that state of mind that can be defined as fascination, enchantment" (TOB 108.8, pp. 558–559).

In this way the language of the body finds a "rich echo" in the bridegroom's words. He speaks in poetic transport and metaphors, which attest to the experience of beauty, to "a love filled with pleasure" (TOB 108.8, p. 559). The bridegroom says, "You are all beautiful, my beloved, and there is no spot in you" (Song 4:7). And further on he calls her "my perfect one" (Song 5:2). John Paul tells us that the bridegroom's desire, "born of love" on the basis of the language of the body, is "a search for integral beauty, for purity free from every stain; it is a search for perfection that contains … *the synthesis of human beauty, beauty of soul and body*" (TOB 112.3, p. 584).

John Paul continues:

> And if the words of the bridegroom just quoted ["Open to me … my perfect one"] seem to contain the distant echo of the "beginning" — that first search-aspiration of the male man for a being still unknown — they resound much nearer in Ephesians where Christ, as Bridegroom of the Church, desires to see his Bride without "spot," desires to see her "holy and immaculate" (Eph 5:27). (TOB 112.3, p. 584)

As Christopher West says:

> In other words, the bridegroom of the Song, like Christ, points us in two directions. He points us back to the beginning, to God's original plan for married love, and to the eschatological future when the marriage of the Lamb will be

consummated. Then the Bride will be made *perfect forever.*
She will shine radiantly — without blemish, wrinkle, or any
such thing (see Eph 5:27). Then, in the marriage of the
Lamb, we will discover the true, integral beauty of everyone
who forms the great communion of saints. It will be a beauty
"free from every stain," a *"beauty of soul and body,"* as John Paul
says. And this dazzling beauty of every human being will be
but a dim reflection, a little glimmer of the beauty of the
Eternal One whom we will behold "face to face." [3]

The bridegroom frequently refers to the bride first of all
as his "sister": "You have ravished my heart, my sister, my
bride, you have ravished my heart with one glance of your
eyes.... How sweet is your love, my sister, my bride!" (Song
4:9–10). Commenting on this language, the Holy Father says
that this way of speaking says much more than if he had
called her by her proper name. These words show how love
reveals the other person. "The fact that in this approach the
feminine 'I' is revealed for the bridegroom as 'sister' — and
that *she is bride* precisely *as sister* — has a particular eloquence" (TOB 109.4, p. 562). These words show that the
bridegroom does not see her as a thing to be appropriated,
but as a *person* to be loved. To be a person "means both 'being
a subject,' but also 'being in relation'" (TOB 109.4, p. 562).
The term "sister" denotes this. It speaks of the two different
ways in which masculinity and femininity "incarnate" the
same humanity, and it speaks of their being in reciprocal relationship. The bridegroom can also be regarded as "brother":
indeed, the bride declares: "O that you were a brother to me,
who nursed at my mother's breast!" (Song 8:1). Recognizing
each other as brother and sister challenges the man to see
whether he is motivated by love, by the sincere gift of self, or
by lust, a desire to gratify himself. The bridegroom accepts

this challenge and gives a spontaneous answer to it (TOB 109.5, p. 564): "Do not stir up, do not awaken the beloved until she wants it!" (Song 8:4).

John Paul says that the "bridegroom's words tend to reproduce ... the history of the femininity of the beloved person; they see her still in the time of girlhood ('We have a little sister, and she still has no breasts')." In this way, his words "embrace her entire 'I,' soul and body, *with a disinterested tenderness*" (TOB 110.2, p. 566). This same tenderness carries through when the term "sister" gives way to the term "bride." The transition from "sister" to "bride" maintains — and it must maintain — the same recognition of her personhood, of her dignity as "sister." In fact, "through marriage man and woman become brother and sister in a special way" (TOB 114.3, p. 594).

From the Holy Father's analysis of the "language of the body," reread in the truth, it follows that spouses redeemed in Christ will never "look" at one another to desire each other, thereby committing "adultery in the heart." This part of TOB deepens our understanding of the truths present in the audiences devoted to God's original plan and to Christ's appeal to the human heart, as was seen earlier, but now the Holy Father deepens what was seen by applying it to the issue of marital spirituality.

The "Language of the Body" and the Defense of Humanae Vitae

Audiences 118–133 are devoted to John Paul II's defense of *Humanae Vitae* (HV). Audiences 118–125 take up *The Ethical Problem*, whereas audiences 126–133 offer an *Outline of Conjugal Spirituality* as found in the teaching of that encyclical.

The Ethical Problem (TOB 118–125)

John Paul II begins by focusing attention on Pope Paul VI's affirmation that there is an inseparable connection between the unitive and procreative meanings of the conjugal act (HV 12). He points out that these words

> concern the moment in the common life of the couple in which the two, by being united in the conjugal act, become "one flesh."... Precisely *in this moment, so rich in meaning*, it is also particularly important that the "language of the body" be reread in the truth. This reading becomes an indispensable condition for *acting in the truth* or for behaving *in conformity with the value and the moral norm*. (118.4, p. 619)

He emphasizes that Paul VI not only recalled the norm (the inseparable connection) but sought to give it "its *adequate foundation*" that is found in the structure and nature of the conjugal act and the nature of the "acting *subjects themselves*" (118.5, p. 619).

In 119 the Pope emphasizes that Paul's teaching in *Humanae Vitae* on the norm and its adequate foundation is rooted in the natural law as understood by the Church and thus corresponding to "*revealed teaching as a whole* as contained *in the biblical sources* (see HV 4)" (119.3, p. 621). In TOB 120 the Pope stresses that in proposing his teaching Pope Paul appealed to the teaching of Vatican II's *Gaudium et Spes*, 51, which affirms there can be no contradiction between divine laws pertaining to the transmission of life and those pertaining to the fostering of conjugal love. In 121 John Paul shows that the Council and *Humanae Vitae* clearly make it evident that responsible parenthood demands the serious practice of the virtue of marital chastity. While including the disposition to avoid causing a pregnancy when there are good reasons for that, and therefore to practice continence, it simultaneously requires *"the disposition ... to increase the family according to the criteria of prudence"* (121.5, pp. 627–628) and to respect the inseparable bond between the unitive and procreative meanings of the conjugal act.

The "Language of the Body" and "Self-mastery"

Next (123) John Paul II shows how the "language of the body" is related to this teaching and the problem of "maintaining the *adequate relationship* between that which is defined as *'domination ... of the forces of nature'* (HV 2) and *'self-mastery'* (HV 21), which is indispensable for the human person" (123.1, p. 630). "The human body," he declares, is

> the means of the expression of man as an integral whole, of the person, which reveals itself through "the language of the body" ... the "language of the body" should *express ... the truth of the sacrament.* By participating in the eternal plan of Love ... the "language of the body" becomes in fact a "prophetism of the body." ... One can say that *Humanae Vitae* carries this truth about the human body in its masculinity and femininity to its final consequences, not only its logical and moral, but also its practical and pastoral, consequences. (123.2, p. 631)

Continuing, he emphasizes: "[T]he unity of the two aspects of the problem — of the *sacramental* (or theological) and the *personalistic* dimension — corresponds to the 'overall revelation of the body.'" He then goes on to affirm:

> [T]he subject of the natural law is man, not only in the "natural" aspect of his existence but also in the integral truth of his personal subjectivity. He is shown to us in revelation as male and female in his full temporal and eschatological vocation ... called by God to be a witness and interpreter of the

eternal plan of Love by becoming the minister of the sacrament, which has "from the beginning" been constituted in the sign of the "union of the flesh." (123.3, pp. 631–632)

He emphasizes that as ministers of the sacrament constituted by consent and perfected by conjugal union "man and woman are called *to express* the mysterious *'language' of their bodies in all the truth that properly belongs to it."*

Why Contraception Is Intrinsically Evil and Why It Violates the "Language of the Body"

In key passages John Paul then develops his central defense of Paul's encyclical and his argument to show why the intentional use of artificial means to deprive the conjugal act of its fruitfulness is intrinsically evil. These passages need to be cited in full:

Man *is person precisely because he possesses himself and has dominion over himself.* Indeed, inasmuch as he is master over himself he can "give himself" to another. And it is this dimension — the dimension of freedom of the gift — that becomes essential and decisive for the "language of the body" in which man and woman express themselves reciprocally in conjugal union. Given that this union is a communion of persons, the "language of the body" must be judged according to the criterion of truth. This is exactly the criterion *Humanae Vitae* recalls....

According to the criterion of this truth, which must be expressed in the "language of the body," the conjugal act "means" not only love, but also potential fruitfulness, and thus it cannot be deprived of its full and adequate meaning by means of artificial interventions. In the conjugal act, it is not licit to separate artificially the unitive meaning from the procreative meaning, because the one as well as the other belong to the innermost truth of the conjugal act. The one is realized together with the other and, in a certain way, the one through the other. This is what the encyclical teaches (see HV 12). Thus, in such a case, when the conjugal act is *deprived of its inner truth* because it is deprived artificially of its procreative capacity, it also *ceases to be an act of love....*

[I]n the case of an artificial separation of these two meanings in the conjugal act, a real bodily union is brought about, but it does not correspond to the inner truth and dignity of personal communion, *"communio personarum."* This communion demands ... that the "language of the body" be expressed reciprocally in the integral truth of its meaning. If this truth is lacking, one can speak neither of the truth of the reciprocal gift of self nor of the reciprocal acceptance of oneself by the person. Such a violation of the inner order of conjugal communion, a communion that plunges its roots into the very order of the person, *constitutes the essential evil of the contraceptive act.* (123.5–7 pp. 632–633)

As noted already, these passages provide us with John Paul II's defense of the teaching of *Humanae Vitae* and his basic argument in TOB to show why contraception is intrinsically evil. I think it is evident that he finds it evil because it intentionally severs the bond between the unitive and procreative meanings of the conjugal act and violates as well the union of love that the conjugal act is meant to express in and through the language of the body; because of contraception husband and wife no longer "give" and "receive" each other — they are not open to the gift of fertility and of new human life but rather refuse to share their fertility with one another, thus not fully "giving" themselves. This teaching is summarized in John Paul's 1981 apostolic exhortation *Familiaris Consortio*, where he writes in number 32:

When couples, by means of recourse to contraception, separate these two meanings that God the Creator has inscribed in the being of man and woman and in the dynamism of their sexual communion, they act as "arbiters" of the divine plan and they "manipulate" and degrade human sexuality — and with it themselves and their married partner — by altering its value of "total" self-giving. Thus the innate language that expresses the total reciprocal self-giving of husband and wife is overlaid, through contraception, by an objectively contradictory language, namely, that of not giving oneself totally to the other. This leads not only to a positive refusal to be open to life but also to a falsification of the inner truth of conjugal love, which is called upon to give itself in personal totality.[4]

The Ethical Regulation of Fertility

TOB 124–125 are concerned with the ethical regulation of births, or ethical recourse to the rhythm of the cycle. This is *not* the old "rhythm method" but rather the practice of periodic continence made possible by our awareness of our own fertility through contemporary methods of what is called natural family planning. In TOB 124, in dealing with the ethical regulation of fertility, John Paul again reflects on *Humanae Vitae*, which approves of the natural regulation of fertility and in this sense responsible fatherhood and motherhood (124.1). He notes that HV 21 requires perfect self-mastery, dominion over instinct and desires, an ascesis, and constant effort (124.2). He then stresses that the encyclical underlines the truth that the ethical regulation of births demands *"behavior with respect to the family and procreation"* and requires spouses to "acquire and possess solid convictions concerning the true values of life and of the family (HV 21)," and continues by summarizing his teaching in *Familiaris Consortio* (that in turn summarized the teaching of the 1980 Synod of Bishops) regarding the "theology of the body" as giving rise to a "pedagogy of the body" (124.3). What *Humanae Vitae*, the Synod of Bishops, and *Familiaris Consortio* ask for in the ethical regulation of births is ultimately the *"practice [of] conjugal chastity."* That is expressed in the *"natural* regulation *of fertility,"* one in conformity with the "natural law,"

> understood here [as] the "order of nature" in the field of procreation inasmuch as it is understood by right reason: this order is the expression of the Creator's plan for the human person ... [so that] the virtuous character of the attitude expressing itself in the "natural" regulation of fertility is determined, *not so much* by faithfulness to an impersonal *"natural law," but to the personal Creator....* The document [HV] certainly presupposes that *biological regularity* ... [urging] competent persons to study it and apply it in a more thorough way, but it always understands such regularity *as the expression of the "order of nature," that is, of the Creator's providential plan,* in the faithful realization of which consists the true good of the human person. (124.6, pp. 635–636)

In 125 the Pope first emphasizes that the ethical regulation of births requires

> that the way of behaving in question corresponds to the truth of the person and thus to the person's dignity.... As a rational and free being, man can and should reread with insight the biological rhythm that belongs to the natural order. He can and should conform himself to it for the sake of exercising "responsible fatherhood and motherhood" ... according to the Creator's plan in the natural order of human fruitfulness. The concept of a morally right regulation of fertility is nothing other than rereading the "language of the body" in the truth. The same "natural *rhythms* immanent in the generative functions" *belong to the objective truth of this language,* which the persons involved should reread in its full objective content. (125.1, pp. 636–637)

He rightly notes that use of "infertile periods" can be abused

> if the couple thereby attempt to evade procreation without just reasons.... This just level needs to be set by taking into account not only the good of one's family and the state of one's health as well as the means of the spouses themselves, but also the good of the society to which they belong, the good of the Church, and even of humanity as a whole. (125.3)

He further points out that *Humanae Vitae* in no way "*aims one-sidedly* at limiting, even less at excluding children; it means also the willingness to welcome a greater number of children. Above all, according to *Humanae Vitae*, 'responsible parenthood' brings about a 'more profound relationship to the objective moral order established by God, of which a right conscience is a faithful interpreter' (HV 10)" (125.3, p. 638).

In the concluding sections of 125.4–7, John Paul is at pains to show that the ethical regulation of fertility, in the thought of Paul VI, requires true spousal love, the virtue of temperance, and a rejection of any utilitarian attitude. The Pope stresses that all these virtues develop mature moral responsibility.

Outline of Conjugal Spirituality (TOB 126–133)

In all of these catecheses, John Paul seeks to analyze and get to the heart of two aspects of the Church's teaching: that concerning the Christian spirituality of the conjugal life and vocation, and that concerning parents and family as found in Paul VI's *Humanae Vitae*. In 126 he focuses on the "power" that according to HV enables spouses to fulfill their glorious vocation. That power is the *love poured into our hearts by the Spirit*. God will give spouses this power if they ask him for it, especially in prayer and the Holy Eucharist. In 127 his point is that the *power of love* enables the spouses to overcome *the power of concupiscence* that falsifies the "language of the body," thus helping them attain the ends of marriage. This love is linked with chastity that in turn is manifested in self-mastery or continence.

In 128 the Pope focuses on continence, or "the *ability to master, control, and orient the sexual drives* and their consequences" (128.1, p. 644). By submitting themselves to each other in love, spouses must show true concern for the truth of the "language of the body." This leads them to realize that continence is not limited to overcoming concupiscent desire but is above all open to the deeper and more mature values integral to the spousal meaning of the body in its masculinity and femininity. Conjugal chastity is then revealed as "*a singular ability* to perceive, love, and realize those meanings of the 'language of the body' that remain completely unknown to concupiscence itself and progressively enrich the spousal dialogue" (128.3, p. 646). As a result of this, the ascesis demanded by continence makes the affective manifestations of spousal love more intense and rich.

In 129 John Paul shows that true continence, far from causing tensions within the person, is "the only *way to free oneself from such tensions.*" It is nothing other than the spiritual effort to express the language of the body not only in the truth but in "the authentic richness of the 'manifestations of affection'" (129.1, p. 647). He distinguishes between "arousal," bodily and sexual in character, and "emotion," centered on the *wholeness* of the other person as personal subject. Arousal seeks to express itself in the form of bodily, sensual pleasure. Thus it tends toward the conjugal act. Emotion, instead, does not itself tend toward that act but limits itself to other "'manifestations of affection,' in which the spousal meaning of the body expresses itself" (129.6, p. 650). Conjugal continence mediates between arousal and emotion and integrates them into chastity. To understand all this as set forth in TOB 129, it helps, I believe, to note that in his earlier work, *Love and Responsibility*, pages 105–117, then Archbishop Wojtyla used the term "sensuality" for "arousal." He used the term "sentiment" or "affectivity" for "emotion." He called both the "raw materials of love," but noted that they need to be integrated into the person. This integration requires the virtue of chastity, of which continence is an integral part. John Paul makes this very clear when, in TOB 130.2, he writes:

> In the conjugal act, the intimate union should bring with itself a particular intensification of emotion, even more, the deep emotional stirring, by the other person.... The distinction between "arousal" and "emotion" revealed in this analysis only proves *the subjective reactive-emotive richness* of the human "I"; this richness excludes any one-sided reduction and allows the virtue of continence to be realized as an ability to direct the manifestation of both arousal and emotion stirred by the reciprocal reactivity of masculinity and femininity. (p. 651)

Thus, as he continues to note in 130, the right way to understand the practice of periodic continence, which, as *Humanae Vitae* 21 insists, demands "self-mastery," is that spouses have the freedom, won by continence, "to direct sensual and emotive reactions in order to allow the *gift* of self to the other 'I' *on the basis of the* mature *possession* of one's own 'I' in its bodily and emotive subjectivity" (130.4, p. 652).

In 131 the Pope stresses that in the sacrament of Marriage the spouses are given a special gift by the Spirit, that of consecrating their lives to Christ and to each other. In this way love is united to conjugal chastity, which, manifested as continence, "realizes the inner order of conjugal life together. Chastity means living in the order of the heart.... At the center of conjugal spirituality, therefore, stands chastity, not only as a moral virtue (formed by love), but equally as a virtue connected with the gifts of the Holy Spirit — *above all with the gift of reverence for what comes from God*" (131.1–2, p. 653). This gift sustains spouses and develops in them "a singular *sensibility for all* that in their vocation and shared life carries *the sign of the mystery of creation and redemption.*" This includes reverence for the conjugal act and its unitive/procreative meanings (131.4, p. 654).

In 132 John Paul develops this theme of reverence for the conjugal act in which the spousal meaning of the body is linked with its procreative meaning. In fact,

> the virtue of conjugal chastity, and even more so the gift of reverence for that which comes from God, shapes the spirituality of the spouses *for the sake of protecting the particular dignity of this act*, this "manifestation of affection," in which the truth of the "language of the body" can be expressed only by safeguarding the procreative potential. (132.2, p. 656)

TOB 133 is a general summation by John Paul II of his defense of *Humanae Vitae.*

CHAPTER 4

Mulieris Dignitatem (The Dignity and Vocation of Women) and *Letter to Families*

Mulieris Dignitatem

This letter, dated on the Feast of the Assumption on August 15, 1988, was written to close the Marian Year that began in the fall of 1987.

Written after Pope John Paul had finished TOB, *Mulieris Dignitatem* in many ways recapitulates and/or develops its major ideas, that is, the meaning of being a human, bodily, sexual person called to love, and enabled to do so in and through union with Christ and his bride the Church.

The letter is divided into nine parts:

1. Introduction (nos. 1–2)
2. Woman-Mother of God (*Theotókos*) (3–5)
3. The Image and Likeness of God (6–8)
4. Eve-Mary (9–11)
5. Jesus Christ (12–16)
6. Motherhood-Virginity (17–22)
7. The Church-The Bride of Christ (23–27)

8. "The Greatest of These Is Love" (28–30)

9. Conclusion (31)

Parts 2 through 8 all in some way embrace and/or develop themes and ideas central to TOB. As will be seen, I believe these parts in particular develop TOB's presentation of the asymmetrical complementarity of man and woman. In my judgment the final part of this apostolic letter, the conclusion, is not directly related to TOB.

Part 1: Introduction

John Paul points out that the 1987 Synod of Bishops recommended "further study of the anthropological and theological bases that are needed in order to solve the problems connected with the meaning and dignity of being a woman and of being a man." This, he said, is essentially "a question of understanding the reason for and the consequences of the Creator's decision that the human being should always and only exist as a woman or a man" (1.3). The "special presence of the Mother of God in the mystery of the Church," he continued,

> makes us think *of the exceptional link between this "woman" and the whole human family.* It is a question here of every man and woman, all the sons and daughters of the human race, in whom from generation to generation a *fundamental inheritance* is realized, the inheritance that belongs to all humanity and that is linked with the mystery of the biblical "beginning": "God created man in his own image, in the image of God he created him; male and female he created them" (Gen 1:27). (2.1)

He then declared:

> This eternal *truth about the human being*, man and woman — a truth which is immutably fixed in human experience — *at*

the same time constitutes the mystery which only in "the Incarnate Word takes on light.".... This [truth] is precisely what is meant to be the common thread running throughout the present document. (2.2–3)

Part 2: Woman-Mother of God (Theotókos) (3–5)

In number 3, the Holy Father reminds us that "the sending of this Son, one in substance with the Father, as a man 'born of woman,' constitutes the culminating and *definitive point of God's self-revelation to humanity*," a self-revelation "*salvific in character.*" He notes that "a woman is to be found *at the center of this salvific event.*" This self-revelation had been "outlined in *the Annunciation at Nazareth.*" With Mary's response, her *"fiat,"* "the Word is truly made flesh," and Mary "attains *a union with God that exceeds* all the expectations of the human spirit" (3.3–5).

He goes on to point out:

[T]hrough her response of faith Mary exercises her free will and thus fully shares with her personal and feminine "I" in the event of the Incarnation. With her *"fiat," Mary becomes the authentic subject* of that union with God which was realized in the mystery of the Incarnation of the Word, who is of one substance with the Father. (4.3)

I find this passage particularly relevant to the issue of male-female complementarity. Although John Paul II immediately notes that "All of God's action in human history at all times respects the free will of the human 'I,'" his point throughout this part of *Mulieris Dignitatem* is to emphasize the unique significance of the "response" of Mary, the woman, to the message she has just "received." It thus seems to me that this passage gives further evidence that while both men and women are summoned to "give" and to "receive," women are so constituted in their femininity as to "receive in a giving way," whereas men are so constituted in their masculinity as to "give in a receiving way." Thus Mary, in receiving the angel's message, gives herself unreservedly to the Lord who has sent Gabriel to her. By so "giving" herself, by so "responding" to the divine message, Mary receives into her womb the Word who now becomes flesh.

John Paul closes his meditations on this beautiful title of Mary — the "Mother of God" — by declaring:

> The dignity of every human being and the vocation corresponding to that dignity find their definitive measure in *union with God*. Mary, the woman of the Bible, is the most complete expression of this dignity and vocation. For no human being, male or female, created in the image and likeness of God, can *in any* way attain fulfillment apart from this image and likeness. (5.4)

This affirmation echoes a key TOB idea, namely, that the dignity and vocation of every human being, male and female, is inscribed initially into the human person as the only bodily being made in the image of the triune God, who is self-giving love. John Paul then turns his attention in part 3 of *Mulieris Dignitatem* specifically to a profound analysis of the Genesis texts relating the story of the creation of man, male and female, in the image and likeness of God.

Part 3: The Image and Likeness of God (6–8)

The titles of this part and its numbered sections bear witness to its close relationship to TOB, especially in numbers 6 and 7. Number 6 is entitled "The Book of Genesis"; number 7, "Person-Communion-Gift"; and number 8, "The Anthropomorphism of Biblical Language."

The Book of Genesis (6)

In this section the Pope affirms that the immutable basis of Christian anthropology, its understanding of what it means to be a human person, is provided by the biblical accounts of creation in Genesis. Genesis 1:27, "God created man in his own image, in the image of God he created him; male and female he created them," unequivocally affirms that man, male and female, was created in the image of God. Moreover, "This image and likeness of God, which is essential for the human being, is passed on by the man and woman, as spouses and parents, to their descendants: 'Be fruitful and multiply, and fill the earth and subdue it' (Gen 1:28)" (6.1).

John Paul goes on to emphasize that Genesis 1:28, if read together with Genesis 2:18–25,

> *helps us to understand even more profoundly* the fundamental *truth* which it contains *concerning man* created as man and woman in the image and likeness of God.... [T]he woman is created by God "from the rib" of the man and is placed at his side as another "I." ... [T]he woman is immediately recognized by the man as "flesh of his flesh and bone of his bones" (cf. Gen 2:23) and for this very reason she is called "woman." In biblical language this name indicates her essential identity with regard to man — *'is-'issah* — something which unfortunately modern languages in general are unable to express: "She shall be called 'woman' (*'issah*) because she was taken out of man (*'is*) (Gen 2:23)." (6.3–4)

In concluding this paragraph the Pope emphasizes, as he had in TOB, that in creating man, male and female, as persons who are equal in dignity as persons and as being made in God's image, God also created *marriage* "as an indispensable condition for the transmission of life to new generations, the transmission of life to which marriage and conjugal love are by their nature ordered: 'Be fruitful and multiply, and fill the earth and subdue it' (Gen 1:28)" (6.5).

Person, Communion, Gift (7)

Number 7 brings out another major theme of TOB, namely, that the "whole of human history" develops on the basis of an "interpersonal 'communion' ... the integration of *"what is 'masculine' and what is 'feminine'"* (7.5). John Paul writes this in light of *Gaudium et Spes's* affirmation that man is the only being in the visible created world whom God willed for himself, and that he can find himself only "through a sincere gift of himself" (7.6–7). Moreover, we can realize that the "model" for this interpretation of the person "is God himself as Trinity, as a communion of Persons." Thus "to say that man is created in the image and likeness of God means that man is called to exist 'for' others, to become a gift," and this applies to every human person (7.7). All of this helps us see that this text reveals to us the spousal meaning of the body and the spousal character of the relationship between persons. In fact, in 7.8, John Paul declares:

> Already in the Book of Genesis we can discern, in preliminary outline, the spousal character of the relationship between persons, which will serve as the basis for the subsequent development of the truth about motherhood, and about virginity, as two particular dimensions of the vocation of women in the light of divine Revelation.

The Anthropomorphism of Biblical Language (8)

In my opinion this section of *Mulieris Dignitatem* is not directly related to themes of TOB, so here I will merely note the Holy Father's major point. He stresses that although God has revealed himself in human language, revealing man as a being made in his image and likeness, thereby showing that God is in some measure "like man," we must remember that biblical language is "analogical" and that the

> *"non-likeness"* which separates the whole of creation from the Creator is *still more essentially true*. Although man is created in God's likeness, God does not cease to be for him the one "who dwells in unapproachable light" (1 Tim 6:16): he is the "Different One," by essence the "totally Other." (8.1)

Part 4: Eve-Mary (9–11)

Number 9 is headed "The 'Beginning' and the Sin"; number 10, "He Shall Rule Over You"; and number 11, "Proto-evangelium."

John Paul begins number 9 by referring to the teaching of *Gaudium et Spes* 13 on the first man's abuse of his freedom, whereby he set himself against God, and man's subsequent fall. The Pope thereby reminds us of the Church's teaching on original sin. He continues by saying:

> The biblical "beginning" — the creation of the world and of man in the world — *contains* in itself *the truth* about *this sin*, which can also be called the sin of man's "beginning" on the earth.... [And in doing so it] reveals what should be called "the mystery of sin," and even more fully, "the mystery of evil" which exists in the world created by God. (9.1)

In paragraph 2, he immediately declares:

> It is not possible to read "the mystery of sin" without making reference to the whole truth about the "image and likeness" to God, which is the basis of biblical anthropology. This truth presents the creation of man as a special gift from the Creator, containing not only the foundation and source of the essential dignity of the human being — man and woman — in the

created world, but also *the beginning of the call to both of them to share in the intimate life of God himself.* In the light of Revelation, *creation likewise means the beginning of salvation history.* It is precisely in this beginning that sin is situated and manifests itself as opposition and negation.

We see here a clear reference to a major theme of TOB, namely that in the context of Genesis 2 and 3 "we witness the moment in which man, male and female, after having broken the original covenant with his Creator, receives the first promise of redemption in the words of the so-called Protoevangelium ... and begins to live *in the theological perspective of redemption.*" As the Pope continues in this key passage, historical man

> participates not only *in the history of human sinfulness* ... but he also participates *in the history of salvation....* He is ... open to the mystery of the redemption realized in Christ and through Christ.... Precisely *this perspective of the redemption of the body guarantees the continuity and the unity* between man's hereditary state of sin and his original innocence, although within history this innocence has been irremediably lost by him. (TOB 4.3, pp. 143–144)

We can see from this the intimate link between numbers 9 ("The 'Beginning' and the Sin") and 11 ("Protoevangelium"). Thus in number 11, John Paul II explicitly refers, in paragraph 1, to the "protoevangelium" found in Genesis 3:15, "I will put enmity between you and the woman, and between your seed and her seed; he shall bruise your head, and you shall bruise his heel." In the text of *Mulieris Dignitatem*, the Holy Father emphasizes

> that the foretelling of the Redeemer contained in these words refers to "the woman." She is assigned the first place in the Protoevangelium as the progenitrix of him who will be the

Redeemer of man. And since the redemption is to be accomplished through a struggle against evil — through the "enmity" between the offspring of the woman and the offspring of him who, as the "father of lies" (Jn 8:44), is the first author of sin in human history — it is also *an enmity between him and the woman.* (11.1)

He then goes on to say: "The words of the Protoevangelium, reread in the light of the New Testament, express well the mission of woman in the Redeemer's salvific struggle against the author of evil in human history" (11.3).

This passage, as noted, recapitulates a theme explicitly developed in TOB. But in *Mulieris Dignitatem* 11.4, John Paul II further develops this theme by reflecting on the emphasis made in the protoevangelium on the *woman*:

It is difficult to grasp why the words of the Protoevangelium place such strong emphasis on the "woman," if it is not admitted that *in her the new and definitive Covenant* of God with humanity *has its beginning*, the *Covenant* in the redeeming blood of Christ. The Covenant begins with a woman, the "woman" of the Annunciation at Nazareth. Herein lies the absolute originality of the Gospel: many times in the Old Testament, in order to intervene in the history of his people, God addressed himself to women, as in the case of the mothers of Samuel and Samson. However, to make his Covenant with humanity, he addressed himself only to men: *Noah, Abraham, and Moses.* At the beginning of the New Covenant, which is to be eternal and irrevocable, there is a woman: the Virgin of Nazareth. It is a *sign* that points to the fact that "in Jesus Christ" *"there is neither male nor female"* (Gal 3:28). In Christ the mutual opposition between man and woman — which is the inheritance of original sin — is essentially overcome. "For you are all *one* in Jesus Christ," Saint Paul will write (Gal 3:28). (*Mulieris Dignitatem*, 11.4)

Thus in 11.4 the Holy Father shows how the conflict, introduced by sin and the concupiscence that had entered the human heart, leading the man to *dominate the woman* and leading her to be *subservient to him* — themes he had taken up both in TOB and in paragraph 10 of *Mulieris Dignitatem*, titled "He Shall Rule Over You" — is overcome through Christ's redemptive act.

Part 5: Jesus Christ (12–16)

Part 5 focuses on Jesus' relationships with women. Its major emphasis focuses on the way, utterly unheard of in Israel, that Jesus unequivocally proclaims the *dignity of women*. Thus in number 15.1, John Paul emphasizes: "*Christ's way of acting, the Gospel of his words and deeds*, is a constant *protest* against whatever offends the dignity of women." Very early in this part, in number 12.4, he notes that in the Israelite tradition "the male 'dominated,' without having proper regard for woman and for her dignity." Then the Pope recapitulates a major theme of TOB, declaring: "*the 'ethos'* of creation [remember that Jesus urges his auditors to go back to the "beginning"] made the basis of the mutual relationships of two people united in marriage. This 'ethos' is *recalled and confirmed by Christ's words*; it is the 'ethos' of the Gospel and of Redemption."

Again, in 15.1, in which John Paul considers women as "guardians of the Gospel message," he also stresses that women feel "liberated" by the truth proclaimed by Christ. They feel "restored to themselves ... loved with 'eternal love,' with a love which finds direct expression in Christ himself." Here I find an indication of the way women, by reason of their femininity, differ complementarily from men. Precisely because they are loved, i.e., receive the gift of love and ultimately receive it from God himself, from the depths of their being they are called to *receive in a giving way*, while men from the depths of their being are summoned to *give themselves in a receiving way*, as Robert Joyce put it so well.

I believe that this idea is brought into the foreground in the Pope's reflections on Jesus' conversation with Martha after the death of Lazarus. When she says that Lazarus would not have died had Jesus been there, our Lord says to her, "I am the resurrection and the life; he who believes in me, though he die, yet shall he live, and whoever lives and believes in me shall never die. Do you believe this?" And she answers, in words that recall what Peter said at Caesarea Philippi, "Yes, Lord; I believe that you are the Christ, the Son of God, he who is coming into the world" (Jn 11:21–27). And Jesus then raises Lazarus from the dead. John Paul says that *"This conversation with Martha is one of the most important in the Gospel"* (15.2). But why? In the paragraphs that follow, John Paul focuses on the typical *feminine "response" of mind and heart* to the truth proclaimed by Christ. In short, he shows that it is characteristic of women, more than of men, to "receive" the word of God and in turn to "give" themselves unconditionally to God and his work. In short, he shows that women are summoned "to give in a receiving way," thereby, in my judgment, deepening and clarifying a key theme of TOB.

Part 6: Motherhood-Virginity (17–22)

In number 17, a preamble as it were to part 6, John Paul II focuses on motherhood and virginity. As "two dimensions of the female vocation," they acquire their full meaning and value in Mary, who as a Virgin became the Mother of the Son of God. Motherhood, usually "the result of mutual 'knowledge' between a man and woman in the marriage union," is here not "the consequence of matrimonial 'knowledge,' but … the work of the Holy Spirit." Since virginity and motherhood coexist in her, she — the Mother of God — "helps everyone — especially women — to see how these two dimensions, these two paths in the vocation of women as persons, explain and complete each other" (17.1).

Number 18, "Motherhood," is especially rich in TOB related matter. For example, John Paul declares in 18.4:

> Motherhood *is linked to the personal structure of the woman and to the personal dimension of the gift*: "I have brought a man into being with the help of the Lord" (Gen 4:1). The Creator grants the parents the gift of a child. On the woman's part, this fact is linked in a special way to "a sincere gift of self." Mary's words at the Annunciation — "Let it be to me according to your word" — signify the woman's readiness for the gift of self and her readiness to accept a new life.

I believe that here the Holy Father deepens his thought from TOB with reference to the complementarity of male and female. This text shows that while males and females in their asymmetrical imaging of God are summoned both to give and to receive, the woman emphasizes giving in a receiving sort of way, for in receiving the child as a gift from God the woman is called upon to "give" herself to the child.

In the final paragraph of number 18, John Paul II affirms that "the man ... always remains 'outside' the process of pregnancy and the baby's birth; in many ways he has to *learn* his own *'fatherhood' from the mother*." Here we return to the "complementarity" of male and female, with the text indicating that the husband/father can "receive" his own fatherhood only by "giving himself" to the wife/mother and their child. I see this as a deepening of a central TOB idea.

This way of understanding male-female complementarity is, in my judgment, further corroborated in number 19.1,

Motherhood in Relation to the Covenant. There John Paul emphasizes that motherhood "*in its personal-ethical sense* expresses a very important creativity on the part of the woman.... The woman's motherhood presents a special call and a special challenge to the man and to his fatherhood." It is also evident, I think, in 19.4, where the Pope emphasizes how blest are those who "hear the word of God and keep it" (Lk 11:25–28). He maintains that is true in particular of Mary, the Mother of God, who is the paradigm of all women. He then declares: "*The motherhood* of every woman ... expresses a profound '*listening to the word of the living God*' and a readiness to 'safeguard' this Word, which is 'the word of eternal life' (cf. Jn 6:68)."

Another key concept of TOB, namely the bond between spousal love in both marriage *and* virginity, is also developed in this part of *Mulieris Dignitatem*. In light of the eschaton and of eschatological hope, John Paul says:

> the meaning of virginity was developed and better understood as a vocation for women too, one in which their dignity, like that of the Virgin of Nazareth, finds confirmation.... The naturally spousal predisposition of the feminine personality finds a response in virginity understood in this way. Women, called from the very "beginning" to be loved and to love, in a vocation to virginity *find Christ* first of all as the Redeemer who "loved until the end" through his total gift of self; *and they respond to this gift with a "sincere gift"* of their whole lives. They thus give themselves to the divine Spouse. (20.4, 6)

Notice that here, too, the Pope emphasizes the "receptivity" of the woman.

Number 21, "Motherhood According to the Spirit" further deepens and enriches this meaning of the receptive character of feminine spousal love. The Holy Father reflects on the nature of spousal love in women who have, in response to Jesus' love, given themselves to Christ as their spouse. He notes that in marriage the readiness to give oneself, although in principle open to all, consists mainly in the love parents give to their children (fathers in their masculine way, mothers in their feminine way). But in virginity, he emphasizes, "this readiness is open *to all people, who are embraced by the love of Christ the Spouse*" (21.1). Later John Paul focuses on the specific convergence of virginity with motherhood. He had earlier shown that this moves analogically from motherhood in the biological/physical sense to the spiritual; he now shows how it moves analogically from virginity to marriage. "The starting point of this second analogy," he writes, "is *the meaning of marriage*. A woman is 'married' either through the sacrament of marriage or spiritually through marriage to Christ. *In both cases marriage* signifies the 'sincere gift of the person' of the bride to the groom. In this way, one can say that the profile of marriage is found spiritually in virginity" (21.3).

Part 7: The Church–The Bride of Christ (23–27)

The principal purpose of this part of *Mulieris Dignitatem* is the Pope's creative and innovative exegesis of the passage in Ephesians 5:22, in which Saint Paul exhorts women to be subject to their husbands. The Pope's point is that this passage must "be understood and carried out in a new way: as a '*mutual subjection out of reverence for Christ*' (cf. Eph 5:21)" (24.2). But this part is also deeply related to major concepts and themes of TOB.

Thus early in this part John Paul reaffirms a principal TOB concept, namely, the sacramentality of marriage. This theme is front and center in TOB 87–93, in which John Paul analyzes Ephesians 5:21–33. The teaching of TOB on this matter is nicely summarized in *Mulieris Dignitatem*, 23.2:

> In this Letter [Ephesians] the author expresses the truth about the Church as the bride of Christ, and also indicates how this truth is *rooted in the biblical reality of the creation of the human being as male and female.* Created in the image and likeness of God as a "unity of the two," both have been called to a spousal love. Following the description of creation in the Book of Genesis (2:18–25), one can also say that this fundamental call appears in the creation of woman, and is inscribed by the Creator in the institution of marriage, which, according to Genesis 2:24, has the character of a union of persons (*"communio personarum"*) from the very beginning. Although not directly, the very description of the "beginning" (cf. Gen 1:27; 2:24) shows that the whole "ethos" of mutual relations between men and women has to correspond to the personal truth of their being.

Number 23.5 develops the theme that "spousal love," which is at the heart of the marriage between man and woman, finds its paradigm in Christ's spousal love for his Church:

> This *image of spousal love* ... finds crowning confirmation in the Letter to the Ephesians (5:23–32).... In Saint Paul's text the analogy of the spousal relationship moves simultaneously in two directions which make up the whole of the "great mystery" (*"sacramentum magnum"*).
>
> The covenant proper to spouses "explains" the spousal character of the union of Christ with the Church, and in its turn this union, as a "great sacrament," determines the sacramentality of marriage as a holy covenant between the two spouses, man and woman. Reading this rich and complex passage, which *taken as a whole is a great analogy,* we must *distinguish* that element which expresses the human reality of

interpersonal relations from that which expresses in symbolic language the "great mystery" which is divine.

In a subsequent passage (24.2), the Pope in my opinion introduces and clarifies another TOB theme, namely the asymmetrical complementarity of man and woman. This refers to the different ways in which they are made in the image and likeness of God. In this text he emphasizes that "the husband is called the 'head' of the wife *as* Christ is the head of the Church; he is so in order to give 'himself up for her' (Eph 5:25), and giving himself up for her means giving up even his own life." The husband — the male — is thus summoned to "give" himself to his wife and in so doing to "receive" her as God's and her gift to him. This is a theme I find emphasized throughout this apostolic letter.

There is something most remarkable, however, about the way in which the Holy Father presents the complementarity of man and woman. This concerns his emphasis on the truth that, in relationship to Christ, *all Christians, men as well as women*, are in some way feminine, i.e., bridally related to Christ. This flows from the truth that Christ is the bridegroom of his bride, the Church, the one who "gives himself up for her." Thus, in a most significant passage, John Paul writes:

> Christ has entered this history and remains in it as the Bridegroom who "has given himself." "To give" means "to become a sincere gift" in the most complete and radical way: "Greater love has no man than this" (Jn 15:13). According to this conception, *all human beings — both women and men — are called* through the Church, *to be the "Bride" of Christ, the Redeemer of the world*. In this way "being the bride," and thus the "feminine" element, becomes a symbol of all that is "human," according to the words of Paul: "There is neither male nor female; for you are all *one* in Christ Jesus." (Gal 3:28) (25.3)

And again,

> … the analogy of spousal love found in the Letter to the Ephesians links what is "masculine" to what is "feminine," since, as members of the Church, men too are included in the concept of "Bride." This should not surprise us, for Saint Paul, in order to express his mission in Christ and in the Church, speaks of the "little children with whom he is again in travail" (cf. Gal 4:19). In the sphere of what is "human" — of what is humanly personal — *"masculinity" and "femininity" are distinct*, yet at the same time they *complete and explain each other*. This is also present in the great analogy of the "Bride" in the Letter to the Ephesians. In the Church every human being — male and female — is the "Bride," in that he or she accepts the gift of the love of Christ the Redeemer, and seeks to respond to it with the gift of his or her own person. (25.4)

Mulieris Dignitatem also develops and enriches TOB's understanding of the *ethos* meant to exist between husband and wife (cf. TOB 34–43). Thus John Paul declares in number 24, paragraph 5:

> *the challenge presented by the "ethos" of the Redemption* is clear and definitive. All the reasons in favor of the "subjection" of woman to man in marriage must be understood in the sense of a "mutual subjection" of both "out of reverence for Christ." The measure of true spousal love finds its deepest source in Christ, who is the Bridegroom of the Church, his Bride.

Part 8: "The Greatest of These Is Love" (28–30)

This part deepens and clarifies another topic closely linked to TOB: the way that women, in their femininity, complement and differ from men as being made "in the image of God." Thus, in number 29, paragraph 2, the Holy Father first reminds us that the calling of woman into existence at man's side as "a helper fit for him" (Gen 2:18) in the "unity of the two," provides the visible world of creatures with particular conditions so that "the love of God may be poured into the hearts" of the beings created in his image.

He immediately declares:

When the author of the Letter to the Ephesians calls Christ "the Bridegroom" and the Church "the Bride," he indirectly confirms through this analogy *the truth about woman as bride.* The Bridegroom is the one who loves. The Bride is loved: *it is she who receives love, in order to love in return.*

The woman, having received love, then gives love to others, first of all to her husband. This clearly affirms that women, in their femininity, are to emphasize "receiving in a giving way," whereas their husbands, in their masculinity, are called to emphasize "giving in a receiving way" inasmuch as their model, Christ the Bridegroom, is the one who gives himself unreservedly to his Bride, the Church.

This entire part shows that women, in their femininity, are indeed those who receive love precisely so that they can give it to others. Women hold a priority in love. This is their mission, their vocation.

Letter to Families

Pope John Paul II's *Letter to Families,* dated February 2, 1994, was written to express the Church's concern for families during the International Year of the Family. It contains an introduction (nos. 1–5) and two major parts:

1. The Civilization of Love (6–17)
2. The Bridegroom Is With You (18–23)

In this letter, the Holy Father speaks passionately about the absolutely indispensable role the family, rooted in the marriage of one man and one woman, has to play in the "civilization of love." His burning desire is to awaken in the hearts and minds of men and women, especially Christian spouses, an understanding of and commitment to the sublime mission God has entrusted to families. The Pope also desires to encourage husbands and wives to be faithful to their vocation, and to defend the family from the dangers threatening it today.

Like *Mulieris Dignitatem*, the Holy Father wrote the *Letter to Families* after he had finished his series of addresses on the theology of the body. This letter does not proceed as systematically as does *Mulieris Dignitatem*. Rather, it summarizes John Paul II's teaching on marriage and the family as presented in his papal writings on this subject. They includes his TOB catecheses, *Familiaris Consortio*, *Mulieris Dignitatem*, and the thousands of homilies and addresses devoted to marriage and family. Thus within the *Letter to Families* we find explicit references to the indissolubility of marriage, the spousal meaning of the body, marriage as the "primordial sacrament," marriage as a sacrament of redemption, the Eucharist and marriage, and the "ethos" of marital love. But my judgment after reading and pondering this letter many times, is that in *Letter to Families*, he does not develop and deepen key ideas and themes of TOB, as he did in *Mulieris Dignitatem*.

Hence I shall provide: (1) a brief summary exposition of the letter's contents; and (2) a more detailed presentation of the major ideas found under different headings in the letter.

Summary of Contents

The document could be summed up as follows: God is a communion of persons; God is love; man was created by God precisely because he wills to share his inner triune life of love with beings other than himself. The innate vocation of man is to love as God loves and to live in a communion of persons. Man and woman image God in complementary ways, and his full image is discovered in their *communio personarum*. This *communio* is fulfilled and perfected through the gift of children. The family community has the task, the mission, of creating a "civilization of love," of serving life and the wider human community. But to carry out this task, the family needs the help of the wider human community (which it is meant to serve). Today, the civilization of love is threatened by the utilitarian, individualistic, neo-Manichaean anti-civilization of death. This must be overcome, and it can be overcome, but only through prayer and through fidelity to God's plan for marriage and human existence.

Major Ideas

Introductory Material

The introductory material (nos. 1–5) includes a discussion of the family as the "way" of the Church, and reflections on prayer. Here the Pope develops two ideas in particular. The first is that *the family is the "way" of the Church* (2–3). The family is the first and most important of the paths that the Church must take in exercising her mission of redemptive service and love. This is so because *man*, whom Christ has entrusted to the Church, owes his existence to the family and goes forth from the family to realize in a new family his personal vocation in life. The family provides each of us with our "existential horizon," inasmuch as it is the fundamental community in which the whole network of our social relationships is grounded. Born from the Creator's love, the family provides the "home" where God's only-begotten Son enters human history in order to reveal man fully to himself, to redeem us and reconcile us to his Father. Finally, the Christian family is truly the "domestic Church."

A second major theme is *the need for prayer* (cf. especially no. 4). John Paul II considers his letter a "prayer" to Christ, asking him to remain in every human family and to dwell in the great human family so all of us can truly say, "Our Father." Prayer, the Pope insists, is necessary to discover human subjectivity, i.e., the depths of the human person as called to communion with God. Prayer, moreover, is necessary for the family because it is a communion of persons and hence has a subjectivity proper to itself.

Part 1: The Civilization of Love

This part, embracing numbers 6–17, is filled with rich ideas clustered around the topics identified in the headings given each number. The following summary of each numbered section paraphrases the text.

6. "Male and female he created them." Man, whom God created male and female, is the only living being on earth made in God's image and likeness. Thus human fatherhood and motherhood bear a unique and essential "likeness" to God; this likeness is the basis of the family as a community of persons united in love. Thus the primordial model of the family is found in the Trinitarian mystery of the divine "we." That is the pattern of the human "we" formed by man and woman made in his image and likeness. God himself wills male and female complementarity.

7. The marital covenant. The family takes its origin in the marital covenant of husband and wife, and is the first and basic expression of our social nature. The family's proper way of living together is communion. Only persons are capable of living in communion, and the primordial human communion is that of husband and wife in marriage. The indissoluble character of the marital union is the basis for the common good of the family. The marital covenant enables spouses to live a lasting communion of love and life, one fulfilled by the procreation of children. God, "from whom every family is named" (Eph 3:15), is the source enabling fathers and mothers to be continually renewed in love. Their fatherhood and motherhood are a sublime task entrusted to them as husband and wife.

8. The unity of the two. Marriage comes into being when a man and woman freely choose to give themselves irrevocably to one another for life. Their marital union bears a likeness to the union of the divine persons and the union of God's children in truth and in love (cf. *Gaudium et Spes*, 24). The capacity and need to live in truth and love is central to human identity. This capacity opens men and women to the communion of marriage, in which they are so closely united that they become one flesh (Gen 2:24). Their union is both spiritual and bodily. Indeed, it is through their bodies that man and woman are predisposed to form a communion of persons in marriage, which Christ has raised to the dignity of a sacrament. The love of husband and wife calls them to cooperate with God in giving life to new human persons.

9. The genealogy of the person. The genealogy of the person is bound up with the family. It is inscribed in the very biology of generation because the new person, born of the conjugal union, brings into the world a new living image of God. Thus God himself is present in fatherhood and motherhood in a unique way. The new person, like his parents, is called to a life in truth and in love. The depths of his being as a person, as the only creature whom God has willed for its own sake (cf.

Gaudium et Spes, 24) are fully revealed only through the Incarnate Word, who shows us that God's will is to lavish upon man a sharing in his own divine life.

10. The common good of marriage and the family. Consent to marriage defines the common good of the couple and of the family. This includes first the common good of the spouses: love, fidelity, honor, and the permanence of their union until death. The good of the parents becomes the good of the children, for the spouses commit themselves to welcome children lovingly and to educate them in love of God and neighbor. Through the genealogy of persons, conjugal communion becomes a communion of persons. The sacramental marriage of Christian spouses, which images the "great mystery" (cf. Eph 5:32) of the life-giving, love-giving union of Christ and the Church, endures and grows stronger by becoming a union in prayer. Since good diffuses itself, the good of the family should reach out to others and share life abundantly.

11. The sincere gift of self. As the only earthly creature God has willed for itself, man finds himself only in the sincere gift of himself to others (cf. *Gaudium et Spes*, 24). In marriage man and woman "give" themselves unconditionally to one another, establishing an indissoluble union. Because Christ died for them, the man and the woman are "gifts" purchased at a great price. In doing so, husband and wife open themselves to the "gift" of a child, a new human person, whose existence is a "gift" of the Creator to the creature. The child is the common good of the family, whose own life becomes a "gift" to his parents, brothers, sisters, and the entire family, which is the place where an individual can exist "for himself" through the sincere gift of self.

12. Responsible fatherhood and motherhood. To promote the dignity of marriage and the family is a duty requiring responsible parenthood, which demands that spouses fully respect the unitive and procreative dimensions of conjugal union. These cannot be intentionally separated without harming the truth of the conjugal act. As a mutual "gift" of husband and wife, the marital act must be "open" both to the gift of conjugal love and to the gift of new human life. This means that spouses must never intentionally impede either love or life when they freely choose to give themselves to one another in the marital embrace.

13. *The two civilizations.* The family, the domestic church, is the center and heart of the civilization of love because of the intensity and closeness of the bonds among its members. The civilization of love, entrusted to men by God, takes its origin in the revelation of God, who is love and who reveals man most fully to himself through Christ, who came to show him the way of love. This civilization requires that man "find himself" through the sincere gift of himself in love. Only then can a true communion of persons flourish. This will overcome "*the possibility of a destructive 'anti-civilization'*, as so many present trends and situations confirm."

14. *Love is demanding.* Precisely because the love celebrated by Saint Paul in 1 Corinthians 13 — the love of God poured into our hearts — is so demanding, it is the source of beauty and of the true good of man. This love, by its nature diffusive, creates the good of persons and communities. This kind of demanding, selfless love is the only true foundation of the family and is the most important dimension of the civilization of love. True freedom requires this love, for freedom is not license. True freedom means giving the gift of self. Personalism is radically different from selfish individualism, for personalism realizes that persons flourish only in a communion of persons, a communion made possible by the gift of self in love.

15. The Fourth Commandment: Honor your father and your mother. This commandment deals with the family in its interior unity, because honor is the safeguard of the family, a community of intense interpersonal relations. The honor due parents is analogous to the worship due God. Honor, which is connected with justice, requires love and is essentially an attitude of unselfishness demanding the sincere gift of self. Parents should live in such a way that they merit their children's honor. Indirectly, this commandment requires parents to honor their children. Honor enables all family members to respect one another and in this way achieve the good of "being together." The civilization of love is not a utopia, but it can be realized if the family is characterized by honor among its members; honor enables family members to lay the social foundations of the civilization of love.

16. Education. Two truths are central to the raising of children: (1) that man is called to live in truth and love; and (2) that everyone finds fulfillment through the sincere gift of self.

The educator "begets" in a true spiritual sense, and education is a true apostolate, one shared by both parents as a gift they "offer" their children. Education begins even before birth, for the mother profoundly influences the child in her womb, and the husband must recognize that his wife's motherhood is a gift. God's fatherhood is the pattern for human fatherhood and motherhood (cf. Eph 3:14–15). Parents, the primary educators of their children, are competent for the task because they are parents. Others involved in the education of children do so only in the name of the parents, with their consent, and to some degree with their authorization. The Church's role in education cannot supplant the primary role of parents. The Church can exercise her role only with the help of parents, who are the first evangelists of their children. Above all, parents must help their children discover their personal vocation and help prepare them for marriage, if that is their vocation.

17. Family and society. Civil society must respect the dignity of marriage and the family and refuse to dignify as "marriage" and accord the same rights to nonmarital unions. Precisely because no society can be permissive in fundamental issues confronting marriage and family, the Church must defend the dignity and rights of marriage and family. The family has a certain kind of sovereignty and is the subject of family rights, closely linked to the rights of persons, which civil society is obligated to recognize and respect. Each "greater" society is conditioned by the family: the nation, in the culture of which the family participates; and the state, which is distinct from the nation and constitutes a political community ordered to the common good. A key social principle is subsidiarity, which means that "greater" societies must respect the proper autonomy and sovereignty of lesser human communities — above all, the family.

Part 2: The Bridegroom Is With You

18. At Cana in Galilee. Jesus, the Bridegroom, is with families (cf. Mt 9:15). By identifying himself as Bridegroom, Jesus, whose first public miracle took place at the wedding feast of Cana (Jn 2:1–11), wishes to make clear to what extent the truth about the family is part of God's revelation and the history of salvation. The Old Testament, in portraying God's love for his people, compared it to the love of husband for wife (cf. Hosea). In the New Testament, Jesus is portrayed as the Bridegroom of the Church, his people. Jesus, the herald of the truth about the family, shows that spousal love, so tender and intimate, gives rise to profound and radical demands, among them indissoluble unity and faithful love between spouses. Although such love is difficult for hearts hardened by sin, it can be realized. It is not utopian, because Jesus himself is with us, with husbands and wives, with their families, and he will never abandon them. Marriage is a vocation, as is the call to embrace celibacy for the sake of God's kingdom. Families need not be afraid! God himself empowers family members to love one another fully and to carry out their glorious mission of serving life and love. Families need to frequent the sacraments, especially the Eucharist and the sacrament of Reconciliation. And all Christians must keep in mind how the sacrament of Confirmation brings baptism to maturity.

19. The Great Mystery. Marriage is a "great mystery" (Eph 5:32), precisely because it expresses the conjugal love of Christ for his Church. Christ's bridal union with the Church brings to fulfillment the love union of God with his people. Christian spouses, who have been washed by the waters of baptism, are united in the sacrament of Marriage. Their union is holy because it both symbolizes and makes present in the world the life-giving, love-giving, grace-giving union of Christ with his Church. The family, as domestic church, is the bride of Christ, who will never abandon Christian husbands and wives. The ultimate meaning of the Fourth Commandment is revealed by Paul in Ephesians, chapter 5. Mutual love and respect between husband and wife, parents and children, are the principles of family stability. Central to the civilization of love is respect, indeed reverence, for the human body, male and female. The body is not an instrument of the person but integral to the person and a revelation of the person. Thus the civilization of love is threatened by dualism and new forms of Manichaeanism.

20. Mother of fairest love. The history of "fairest love" begins with the Annunciation, because Mary is the mother of fairest love. Joseph was truly her husband, and thanks to him the mystery of the Incarnation and the mystery of the Holy Family come to be profoundly inscribed in the spousal love of husband and wife. If love is to be "fairest love," it must come from the one who is himself a gift and the source of every gift. Love and beauty go hand in hand and are fully revealed in the Incarnation, which is the source of a new beauty in the history of mankind. Mary and Joseph are models of "fairest love," which requires chastity and the overcoming of concupiscence, through which man tends to treat other human beings as his own possession.

21. Birth and danger. The birth of Jesus was marked by danger: Simeon predicted that a sword would pierce Mary's heart (Lk 2:32–35), and Herod plotted the child's death. These facts have a certain prophetic eloquence. They show that the proclamation of life, so central to the Gospel and the civilization of love, is faced with threats. The truth about man today is particularly endangered. Indeed, today a "civilization of death" reigns in the hearts of many. Thus the conscience of people must be reawakened to the truth about man.

22. "You welcomed me." We must be born anew (Jn 3:6–7) to prepare ourselves to welcome our Bridegroom, Jesus. Christian husbands and wives are the first witnesses and servants of this rebirth in the Holy Spirit. They must remember that the life they beget is begotten for God, for eternal life with the Blessed Trinity. Christ will judge us in the light of the persons we have made ourselves to be through our free choices, which should be made in the light of love of God and of the human persons made in his image, whose inviolable goods are protected by the precepts of the Decalogue. The judge is the Bridegroom of the Church and of humanity, and he wants us to welcome him by welcoming into our hearts and homes his brothers and sisters, the men and women whose nature he shared so intimately so that they could share his. His agony at Gethsemane and on Calvary reveals the depths of his love for us.

23. *"Be strengthened in the inner man."* The family, fatherhood, and motherhood go hand in hand. The family is the first human setting in which the "inner man" of whom Paul speaks is formed (cf. Eph 3:16), the man who must be strengthened in the Spirit. In our pilgrimage on earth, we must make the Holy Family our model, for from it Jesus the Bridegroom proclaims the gospel of the family. The history of mankind, of salvation, passes through the family, to which is entrusted the task of unleashing the forces of good. The family must be strong with the strength of God.

Thus it is evident, I believe, that *Mulieris Dignitatem* both recapitulates and develops specific themes and concepts of the theology of the body, whereas the *Letter to Families*, more general in scope and purpose, does neither of those things directly.

Notes

Introduction

1. Karol Wojtyla, *Love and Responsibility* (New York: Farrar, Straus, and Giroux, 1981; reprinted 1993, Ignatius Press).

2. Pope John Paul II, *Man and Woman He Created Them: A Theology of the Body*. Translation, introduction, and index by Michael Waldstein. (Boston: Pauline Books & Media, 2006), p. 79.

3. Ibid.

4. Christopher West, *The Theology of the Body Explained: A Commentary on John Paul II's "Gospel of the Body"* (Boston: Pauline Books & Media, 2007).

CHAPTER 2

Familiaris Consortio (The Role of the Christian Family in the Modern World) and the Theology of the Body

1. Pontifical Council for the Family, *Charter of the Rights of the Family*, October 22, 1983. See http://www.catholic.com/library/crf_charter_rights_fam1.asp.

2. For this section I have summarized material presented at greater length in an article I wrote with my wife, Patricia A. May; "The Family as a Saved and Saving Community: A Specific and Original Ecclesial Role," in *The Christian Family in the World Today: Proceedings of the 16th Convention of the Fellowship of Catholic Scholars* (Steubenville, OH:

Convention of the Fellowship of Catholic Scholars (Steubenville, OH: Franciscan University Press, 1994), pp. 179–201.

Chapter 3

John Paul II's Catecheses on the Theology of the Body: "Man and Woman He Created Them"

1. This chapter is a revised and expanded version of previously published material. Substantive portions published in *Marriage: The Rock on Which the Family Is Built*, revised 2009 edition, Ignatius Press, and used here with permission.

2. Robert Joyce, *Human Sexual Ecology: A Philosophy and Ethics of Man and Woman* (Washington, D.C.: University Press of America, 1980), p. 70ff. See also William E. May, *Marriage: The Rock on Which the Family Is Built*, 2nd ed. (San Francisco: Ignatius Press, 2009), chapter 2, "Marriage and the Complementarity of Male and Female."

3. West, *The Theology of the Body Explained*, p. 480.

4. Other arguments show that contraception is intrinsically evil, in particular:

(1) Karol Wojtyla's argument in *Love and Responsibility* in which he holds that whenever a man and a woman freely choose to engage in genital sex, they should be willing to become fathers and mothers (and to do so they ought to be married to one another). Obviously they are not so willing if they choose to contracept the freely chosen genital act.

(2) The argument that contraception is an antilife act akin to homicide, an argument set forth in the "si aliquis" operative in canon law from the twelfth century until 1917. It is also found in the teaching of the *Roman Catechism* (the *Catechism of the Council of Trent*) in its teaching on marriage, a teaching explicitly referred to by Paul VI in *Humanae Vitae*, no. 14, n. 16, and developed fully by Germain Grisez, Joseph Boyle, John Finnis, and William E. May in their essay, "'Every Marital Act Ought to Be Open to New Life': Toward a Clearer Understanding," The Thomist 52.3 (1988), 365–426; published in Italian under the title, "'Ogni atto coniugale deve essere aperto a uno nuova vita': verso una comprensione più precisa," in *Anthropotes: rivista di studi sulla persona e la famiglia* 4.1 (May 1988), 73–122.

BOOKS & MEDIA

The Daughters of St. Paul operate book and media centers at the following addresses. Visit, call or write the one nearest you today, or find us on the World Wide Web, www.pauline.org

CALIFORNIA

3908 Sepulveda Blvd, Culver City, CA 90230	310-397-8676
2460 Broadway Street, Redwood City, CA 94063	650-369-4230
5945 Balboa Avenue, San Diego, CA 92111	858-565-9181

FLORIDA

145 S.W. 107th Avenue, Miami, FL 33174	305-559-6715

HAWAII

1143 Bishop Street, Honolulu, HI 96813	808-521-2731
Neighbor Islands call:	866-521-2731

ILLINOIS

172 North Michigan Avenue, Chicago, IL 60601	312-346-4228

LOUISIANA

4403 Veterans Memorial Blvd, Metairie, LA 70006	504-887-7631

MASSACHUSETTS

885 Providence Hwy, Dedham, MA 02026	781-326-5385

MISSOURI

9804 Watson Road, St. Louis, MO 63126	314-965-3512

NEW YORK

64 W. 38th Street, New York, NY 10018	212-754-1110

PENNSYLVANIA

9171-A Roosevelt Blvd, Philadelphia, PA 19114	215-676-9494

SOUTH CAROLINA

243 King Street, Charleston, SC 29401	843-577-0175

VIRGINIA

1025 King Street, Alexandria, VA 22314	703-549-3806

CANADA

3022 Dufferin Street, Toronto, ON M6B 3T5	416-781-9131

¡También somos su fuente para libros,
videos y música en español!